The Phantom of the Opera

GASTON LEROUX

Level 5

Retold by Coleen Degnan-Veness
Series Editors: Andy Hopkins and Jocelyn Potter

Pearson Education Limited
Edinburgh Gate, Harlow,
Essex CM20 2JE, England
and Associated Companies throughout the world.

ISBN: 978-1-4058-6515-9

First published by Penguin Books 2002
This edition published 2008

5 7 9 10 8 6 4

Text copyright © Penguin Books Ltd 2002
This edition copyright © Pearson Education Ltd 2008

Typeset by Graphicraft Ltd, Hong Kong
Set in 11/14pt Bembo
Printed in China
SWTC/04

Published by Pearson Education Ltd in association with
Penguin Books Ltd, both companies being subsidiaries of Pearson Plc

For a complete list of the titles available in the Penguin Readers series please write to your local
Pearson Longman office or to: Penguin Readers Marketing Department, Pearson Education,
Edinburgh Gate, Harlow, Essex CM20 2JE, England.

Contents

Introduction

"The Opera ghost!" Jammes screamed in terror; and her finger pointed, among the crowd, to a face so ugly, so pale, with two deep black holes for eyes.

"The Opera ghost! The Opera ghost!"

The managers of the Paris Opera, Monsieur Poligny and Monsieur Debienne, have had enough of this ghost, so they are retiring. The new managers, Monsieur Richard and Monsieur Moncharmin, have a choice: do what the ghost wants or suffer his revenge.

But is there really a phantom in the opera house? Madame Giry, the box-keeper, is sure there is. She has never seen him, but she hears him. And the managers receive letters from O.G., who demands that they keep Box Five for his use only. The new managers think it is all a joke until they can find no other explanation for some mysterious events.

Many years after these events, which excited the Paris upper classes at the time, the historian telling the story visited the National School of Music. He spent hours reading letters, papers, and Monsieur Moncharmin's *A Manager's Memories*. He spoke to many people, including the detective on the case and "the Persian," who knew more than anybody. In *The Phantom of the Opera* we learn what the historian discovered.

Gaston Leroux was born in Paris in 1868, and his life was as interesting as his stories. In his own time he was a celebrated journalist, an international adventurer, and one of the most popular writers of mysteries and horror stories in the whole world. Photographs show him as a fashionably dressed, rather fat man with oily dark hair and a moustache.

From a young age, Gaston wanted to become a writer, and with this as his goal, he was an excellent student who wrote poetry and short stories for his own pleasure. But when his father, a wealthy storeowner, decided that his son should be a lawyer, Gaston changed from an enthusiastic student to a very lazy one. His great love was the theater, and it is not surprising that after he finally received his law degree in 1889 and began working as a lawyer, he continued to write in his spare time. His father's sudden death in 1889 changed the direction of Gaston's life; he gave up the law and had a wild time, enjoying the pleasures offered by late-nineteenth-century Paris. Unsurprisingly, he lost all of the fortune his father had left him within a year.

Even without money, Leroux refused to be discouraged. In 1890 he got a job on the newspaper *L'Echo de Paris* and became a full-time journalist. His work reporting on the courts and the theater combined his knowledge of the law and love of the theater. He especially enjoyed examining illegal practices in the police force and among government officials. His reports on these subjects made him famous as a newspaperman in Paris; his name on a story guaranteed big sales of that day's newspaper.

With his taste for adventure and danger, the young reporter began to travel. Between 1894 and 1906, he witnessed wars and other important events in places as different as Sweden, Finland, Egypt, and Korea. In 1905 he was in Morocco dressed as an Arab and was able to talk to people about important political events at a time when France and Germany were struggling for power in that country. He also traveled to Russia, where he learned about the big political and social changes going on there.

During those years of traveling, Leroux wrote four novels and eventually gave up foreign adventure and political journalism for the life of a novelist in England. His early works show that he was interested in the writing of Alexandre Dumas and Victor Hugo. Between the years 1903 and 1927 he produced two dozen books which appeared one chapter at a time in newspapers, many shorter works, and seven plays. In Britain and the United States, he was well known as a mystery writer who wrote exciting books full of blood and violence.

Leroux's first big success, *The Mystery of the Yellow Room*, came out in 1907. In this novel he introduced his young crime reporter and detective, Joseph Rouletabille, who solved the mystery of a crime committed inside a locked room. In its time, this novel was considered the best example of a logical detective story. Rouletabille appeared in several more of Leroux's books as well as in several movies and in a television series in France in the 1960s. The young detective reminds readers of G.K. Chesterton's Father Brown and Agatha Christie's Miss Marple. He also reminds readers of Arthur Conan Doyle's Sherlock Holmes because he has a friend named Sinclair who is similar to Holmes's Dr. Watson. Besides the detective stories, Leroux wrote more horror stories, including *La Double Vie de Theophrastes Longuet* (*The Double Life of Theophrastes Longuet*) and *La Reine du Sabbat* (*The Queen of Sabbat*).

Gaston Leroux's private life continued to be almost as exciting as his fiction. He married his wife before the turn of the century and stayed married to her, but from 1902 he lived openly with another woman. He moved from Paris to Nice and enjoyed spending his money; he was always confident that he could write another book and pay his bills. Friendly and sociable, he also had a darker side which explained his interest in death, horror, and the spirit world.

In Paris in 1910, the book that Leroux is most remembered for appeared in print: *Le Fantôme de l'Opéra* (*The Phantom of the Opera*). In the introduction to *The Phantom*, the author explains how he found out about the strange events in the 1880s at Paris's famous opera house. The Paris Opera was built between 1861 and 1875 to designs by Charles Garnier and covered a very big piece of land. The ground was wet since there was an underground lake, and large amounts of water had to be pumped out to dig the deep cellars over which the Opera was built.

As a journalist, Leroux reported on performances at the Opera, and he was able to explore parts of the building that the public never saw. He even visited the underground lake and saw skeletons there. He described for his readers in great detail the hundreds of rooms and long passages. There are seventeen floors to the building, five of which are underground. The mysteries behind the 2,500 doors and many trap doors excited his imagination, especially at the end of the nineteenth century when people everywhere in Europe were very interested in the spirit world and in ghosts and phantoms.

At the time in which the novel is set, the Opera House employed more than fifteen hundred people and had space to keep a number of white horses under the entranceway, ready for the use of the opera company. Today the Opera is still an extraordinary building, and it has more or less the same form that it had in 1910. It employs more than a thousand people and houses two permanent ballet schools. And, there really is a lake underneath the building. There could be no better scene for *The Phantom of the Opera*.

The idea for the Phantom story is familiar to readers as the traditional, tragic story of an ugly creature who falls in love with a beautiful young girl. The terrible creature becomes gentle because the girl shows kindness and understanding towards him. In Leroux's book, the Phantom is intelligent and very talented but also violent and evil. He does not have a place in normal society because he is very ugly; he must wear a mask to cover his awful face, and he must live in the shadows. He tricks Christine (the young opera singer) and makes her part of his secret life by teaching her to sing more beautifully than anyone else in Paris, but, of course, evil cannot win in the end. Leroux tells us a wonderful story about the struggles between ghosts, angels, and lovers.

Even with this background, the book was not enthusiastically received at first and sales of *The Phantom* were only average. But then the story came out chapter-by-chapter in French, English, and American newspapers and included frightening drawings of the Phantom and his underground world. The book suddenly became an international success.

Producers at a big Hollywood film company found out about the story and made the first film of *The Phantom of the Opera* in 1925. It was a silent movie starring Lon Chaney, an American actor known as "The Man of a Thousand Faces." Chaney's amazing performance made the story even more famous around the world and led to many more plays and films based on Gaston Leroux's story. Since 1987, the most famous *Phantom of the Opera* has been Andrew Lloyd Webber's musical-theater production. It continues to be seen on stages everywhere and has been made into a movie.

Leroux also wrote stage plays, mostly based on his own books. He wrote for movies, and in 1919 he formed his own production company, called Cinéromans. From 1909 Leroux wrote a book a year until his death at the age of fifty-nine. By that time, he had achieved a reasonable level of fame and lived in a beautiful home which he had named "The Palace of the North Star." Tragically, he did not live long enough to see the great success of his Phantom story, although it is believed that he saw the Lon Chaney movie in 1926.

When Gaston Leroux died after surgery on April 15, 1927, he had written more than sixty novels, but he would probably be surprised to know that during the last century, his Phantom has been seen on movie and television screens and in theaters around the world. There have been eighteen films and nine theatrical productions based on the story. The 1925 *Phantom* is even available today on DVD. And, of course, you can find more information and discussion groups on the Internet. We can be confident that all of this would make Gaston Leroux, the former journalist and great theater-lover, very happy.

Chapter 1   Is It the Ghost?

It was the evening on which Monsieur* Debienne and Monsieur Poligny, the managers of the Opera, were giving a last performance to mark their retirement. Suddenly, a half dozen young ladies of the ballet were in the dressing room of La Sorelli, one of the main dancers. Some were laughing unnaturally and some were screaming in terror. Sorelli, who wished to be alone for a moment to practice her speech to the departing managers, looked around angrily at the noisy crowd. It was Jammes who gave the explanation in a shaky voice: "It's the ghost!" And she locked the door.

Sorelli was superstitious. When she heard this, she called the fifteen-year-old Jammes a "silly little fool" but then asked for details. "Have you seen him?"

"As clearly as I see you now!" said Jammes.

Then little Giry added, "He's very ugly!"

"Oh, yes!" cried the other girls.

They all began to talk together. The ghost had appeared to them in the shape of a gentleman in fine clothes. He suddenly stood in front of them in the passage and seemed to have come straight through the wall.

"Oh, you see the ghost everywhere!" said one of them, who had remained more sensible.

And it was true. For several months, all the discussion at the Opera had been of this ghost in fine clothes who walked quietly and slowly around the building. He spoke to nobody and nobody dared speak to him. He disappeared as soon as he was seen. At first, everybody laughed about him, but the story of the ghost

---

* Monsieur: the French word for Mr.

1

soon swelled enormously among the *corps de ballet*.★ All the girls pretended that they met this phantom often. And those who laughed the loudest were the least comfortable.

And who had seen him? You meet so many men in fine clothes at the Opera who are not ghosts. But his suit covered a skeleton. At least, the ballet girls said so. And, it had the face of Death.

Was all this serious? In fact, the idea of the skeleton came from the description of the ghost given by Joseph Buquet, who was in charge of moving scenery. He had really seen the ghost—on the stairs that led to the cellars—for a second before the ghost ran away.

Buquet told his listeners, "He is extraordinarily thin and his coat hangs on his skeleton. His eyes are very deep—just two big, black holes. His nasty yellow skin is tightly stretched across his bones, and he has no nose, which is a horrible thing to look at."

Joseph Buquet was a serious man, not one who imagines things. His words were received with interest and amazement; and soon other people claimed to have seen the ghost. And then, a series of curious events that nobody could explain made everybody feel uncomfortable.

But we must return to the evening when Jammes cried, "It's a ghost!" After the first excitement, everything was quiet in the dressing room. Then, with real terror on her face, Jammes cried, "Listen!"

They could hear somebody outside the door. Sorelli went up to it and in a shaky voice asked, "Who's there?" But nobody answered. Feeling all eyes on her, she asked loudly, "Is anyone behind the door?"

"Oh, yes. Of course there is!" cried little Meg Giry. She held Sorelli back by her skirt. "Whatever you do, don't open the door!"

★ *corps de ballet*: the dancers in a ballet company.

But Sorelli turned the key and opened the door. She bravely looked into the passage. It was empty. The dancer closed the door again.

"No," she said, "there is no one there. Now, girls, stop all this. No one has ever seen the ghost."

"Yes, yes, we saw him—we saw him just now!" cried the girls. "He had his face of Death and his fine clothes, just as when he appeared to Joseph Buquet!"

"And Gabriel, the singing master, saw him, too!" said Jammes. "Gabriel was in the stage manager's office and the Persian came in. Gabriel saw the ghost behind the Persian! He saw the ghost with the face of Death, just like Joseph Buquet's description!"

Little Giry said, "Joseph Buquet should keep quiet."

"Why?" somebody asked.

"That's mother's opinion," replied Meg. She lowered her voice and looked around.

"And why is it your mother's opinion?" asked another girl.

"Mother says the ghost doesn't like being talked about."

"And why does your mother say so?"

All the girls came closer. "Because . . . because . . . I swore not to tell!"

They promised to keep her secret and Meg was desperate to tell all she knew. With her eyes on the door, she began, "Well, it's because of the private box."

"What private box?"

"The ghost's box!"

"Does the ghost have a box in the Opera?"

"Not so loud!" said Meg. "It's Box Five."

"Oh, nonsense!"

"I tell you it is. Mother's in charge of it. No one has had it for over a month, except the ghost, and orders have been given at the box office that it must never be sold."

"And does the ghost really come there?"

"Yes. The ghost comes, but nobody can see him."

"Somebody must see him!"

"All that talk about his fine clothes and his face is nonsense. Mother has never seen him, but she has heard him."

Sorelli grew impatient and little Giry began to cry.

"If mother learns that I have told you ... But I was right— Joseph Buquet was wrong to talk about things that don't concern him. It will bring bad luck—mother was saying that last night ..."

There was a sound of hurried footsteps in the passage and a breathless voice cried, "Jammes! Jammes! Are you there?"

"It's mother's voice," said Jammes. "What's the matter?"

She opened the door. A respectable lady, large and strong, burst into the dressing room and dropped into an empty chair.

"What is it?" the girls cried.

"Joseph Buquet is dead!"

Everybody held their breath, then their shouts and questions filled the air.

"He was found hanging in the third cellar."

"It's the ghost!" cried little Giry, but at once she corrected herself and her little hands covered her mouth. "No, no! I didn't say it!"

Her friends all said quietly, "Yes, it must be the ghost!"

Sorelli was very pale. "I will never be able to give my speech," she said.

In fact, no one ever knew how Joseph Buquet met his death. In his book, *A Manager's Memories*, Monsieur Moncharmin, one of the two managers who ran the Opera after Monsieur Debienne and Monsieur Poligny left, described what happened as follows:

A serious accident spoiled the little party which Monsieur Debienne and Monsieur Poligny gave to celebrate their retirement. I was in the manager's office when Mercier, the scenery manager, suddenly came in. He seemed half mad and told me that the body of a man had been found hanging under the stage. By the time I rushed down the stairs, the man was no longer hanging from his rope!

So, a man hangs at the end of a rope; they go to cut him down; the rope has disappeared. Monsieur Moncharmin found a simple explanation:

It was just after the ballet, and the dancing girls knew they had to hurry and destroy the rope if they wanted to avoid any bad luck because they were very superstitious.

Imagine the *corps de ballet* hurrying down the stairs and dividing the rope among themselves! I think that somebody wanted that rope to disappear as soon as it had done its work.

Sorelli was on her way to give her speech, with all the girls following closely behind, when she ran into Count Chagny, who was coming upstairs.

"I was just going to you," he said, taking off his hat. "Sorelli, what an evening! And Christine Daaé: What a triumph!"

"Six months ago, she used to sing like a chicken," said Meg Giry. "But let us pass, my dear count. We are going to inquire about a poor man who was found hanging by the neck."

Just then Mercier came hurrying past and stopped when he heard this remark. "What?" he asked. "Have you girls heard already? Please, don't let Monsieur Debienne and Monsieur Poligny hear about it. It would upset them too much on their last day."

Count Chagny was right; no performance had ever equaled this one. Christine Daaé had shown her true talent for the first time to the surprised and enthusiastic audience. There were many famous pieces beautifully sung by the famous singers of the day, but Christine Daaé had been, without exaggeration, the best. Her voice produced divine sounds in the prison scene of

Faust★ when she sang in place of La Carlotta, who was sick. No one had ever heard or seen anything like it.

People wanted to know why Daaé, a real jewel, had been kept from them. Why was Daaé only allowed to perform this piece when La Carlotta was sick? Were Debienne and Poligny *trying* to keep this great talent hidden? Why? And why had *she* kept it hidden? The whole thing was a mystery.

Philippe Georges Marie, Count of Chagny, was forty-one, good-looking, and wealthy. Standing up in his box, he had listened to the enthusiastic audience and joined in by clapping loudly. Next to him was his brother, Raoul, who was twenty years younger. Their parents had died when Raoul was very young, so Philippe brought up the young viscount, who later joined the navy. Raoul had just come back from a trip around the world and was now home for six months before his next journey to the North Pole.

Philippe wanted Raoul to see Paris, so he took him everywhere and introduced him to the Opera. On that evening, Philippe was clapping loudly when he looked at his brother, who seemed quite pale. Christine Daaé had just been carried off after fainting at the end of her performance.

"You are not going to faint, too, are you?" Philippe asked.

But Raoul recovered and stood up. "Let's go and see her," he said. "She never sang like that before."

Raoul led the way, feeling that his heart no longer belonged to him, his face a picture of burning desire. Count Philippe followed him through the crowd of gentlemen, scene movers, and ballet girls. When they arrived at Christine Daaé's dressing room, the doctor was there with her—and with a great admiring crowd.

"Don't you think, Doctor, that those gentlemen had better clear the room?" asked Raoul coolly. "She can't breathe here."

"You're quite right," said the doctor.

★ *Faust*: an opera by Gounod.

And, thinking that the young man had a right to stay, he sent everyone away, except Raoul and a servant-woman. She did not know Raoul—in fact, she had never seen him before—but she did not dare to question him.

Christine Daaé turned, looked at the doctor, and smiled. Then, she saw Raoul and asked, "Monsieur, who are you?"

"Mademoiselle,"* replied the young man, kneeling on one knee and pressing a kiss on her hand, "I am the little boy who went into the sea to rescue your scarf."

Christine again looked at the doctor and the servant-woman, and all three began to laugh.

Raoul turned very red and stood up. "Mademoiselle," he said, "since you choose not to recognize me, I would like to say something to you in private, something very important."

"When I am better, do you mind?"

"Yes, you must go," said the doctor, with his pleasant smile. "Let me take care of mademoiselle."

Suddenly, Christine stood up with strange and unexpected energy and asked all the men to leave. Outside her door, the doctor said to Raoul, "She is not herself tonight. She is usually so gentle."

Raoul stood alone after the doctor left. This part of the theater was now empty. He felt a terrible pain in his heart, and this was what he wanted to speak to her about. The servant-woman came out and Raoul asked about Christine. The woman said that she was quite well, but that he must not bother her because she wished to be left alone. Only one idea filled Raoul's burning brain: of course, she wanted to be left alone *for him!* He had told her that he wanted to speak to her privately.

He went to her door and prepared to knock. But his hand dropped. He heard *a man's voice* in the dressing room, saying,

---

* Mademoiselle: the French word for Miss.

"Christine, you must love me!" And Christine's sad voice replying, "How can you talk like that? *When I sing only for you!*"

Raoul's heart beat so loudly that he was sure they would hear it inside. They would open the door and he would be sent away! What a position for a Chagny! To be caught listening behind a door! He put his hands on his heart to make it stop.

The man's voice spoke again. "Are you very tired?"

"Tonight I gave you my soul, and I am dead!" Christine replied.

"Your soul is a beautiful thing, child," replied the man, "and I thank you. No king ever received such a wonderful gift. *The angels in Heaven cried tonight.*"

Raoul heard nothing after that, but he did not go away. He decided to wait until the man left. To his great surprise, the door opened and Christine Daaé appeared, alone. She closed the door behind her, but she did not lock it. Raoul did not even watch her go. His eyes were on the door, but it did not open again.

Raoul let himself in and closed the door. The dressing room was dark. "There is someone here!" said Raoul. "What are you hiding for? You will not leave this room until I let you! If you don't answer, you are a coward. And I will tell everyone!"

Raoul lit a match, and the flame lit up the room. There was no one! "Am I going mad?" he asked, aloud.

He went out, not knowing what he was doing or where he was going. He found himself at the bottom of some stairs and some workmen were coming down behind him, carrying a long board, covered with a white sheet.

"Which is the way out?" he asked one of the men.

"Straight in front of you. But let us pass."

Pointing to the white sheet, he asked, "What's that?"

A workman answered, "That is Joseph Buquet, who was found in the third cellar, hanging."

Raoul took off his hat and let the workmen pass.

Chapter 2   Box Five

During this time, the retirement ceremony was taking place. The most important people in the social and artistic world of Paris had met in the entrance hall of the Opera after the performance. Sorelli waited for the arrival of the retiring managers with a prepared speech at the tip of her tongue. Behind her, the members of the *corps de ballet*, young and old, discussed the events of the day in whispers.

Everybody remarked that the retiring managers looked cheerful. They were smiling broadly as Sorelli spoke—until everyone heard a sudden shout from that little devil, Jammes.

"The Opera ghost!" Jammes screamed in terror; and her finger pointed, among the crowd, to a face so ugly, so pale, with two deep black holes for eyes.

"The Opera ghost! The Opera ghost!"

Everybody laughed and pushed and wanted to offer the Opera ghost a drink, but he was gone. He slipped through the crowd. Some looked for him without success, while two old gentlemen tried to calm little Jammes, and little Giry stood screaming uncontrollably.

Sorelli was very angry that she had not been able to finish her speech. The managers kissed her, thanked her, and ran away as fast as the ghost himself. No one was surprised because there were two more floors above with crowds waiting to say goodbye to them. On the top floor there were personal friends and a wonderful supper.

Here they found the new managers, Monsieur Armand Moncharmin and Monsieur Firmin Richard. The retiring managers had already handed over the two tiny keys which opened all the doors—thousands of doors—of the opera house. Some of the guests noticed, at the end of the table, that strange face with the hollow eyes.

There the ghost sat as naturally as any man. But he neither ate nor drank. No one smiled, or joked, or shouted, "The Opera ghost!" Those who had seen him first and smiled were now turning their heads away.

He did not speak, and the people next to him could not say at what exact moment he had sat down between them. The friends of the new managers thought that this guest was a friend of the old managers. And the friends of the old managers thought that he was a friend of the new managers. So, there was no request for an explanation.

A few of those present who knew the story of the ghost and the description of him by Joseph Buquet thought that the man at the end of the table might be him. But, according to the story, the ghost had no nose and this person had. But Monsieur Moncharmin says in his *Memories* that you could see through the guest's nose. I will add that this might very well be true of a false nose, made for people who have lost their noses naturally or as a result of an operation.

Did the ghost really take a seat at the managers' supper table that night, uninvited? And can we be sure that the figure there was the Opera ghost? I mention it because it seems so strange. And, it is impossible, isn't it?

Moncharmin, in chapter eleven of his *Memories*, says:

When I think of this first evening, I cannot separate the secret told to us by Monsieur Debienne and Monsieur Poligny in their office from the presence of that ghostly person who none of us knew.

This is what happened: Monsieur Debienne and Monsieur Poligny had not seen the man with the face of Death. Suddenly, the man began to speak. "The ballet girls are right," he said. "The death of that poor Buquet is maybe not as natural as people think."

"Is Buquet dead?" they cried.

"Yes," replied the man, or the shadow of a man, quietly. "He was found this evening, hanging in the third cellar."

The two retiring managers rose and stared strangely at the speaker. They were very excited and both men turned white. Monsieur Debienne made a sign to Monsieur Richard and Monsieur Moncharmin; Monsieur Poligny excused himself and the other three men. They went into the managers' office.

I shall leave Monsieur Moncharmin to complete the story. In his *Memories*, he says:

Monsieur Debienne and Monsieur Poligny seemed to grow more and more excited, and they appeared to have something very difficult to tell us. First, they asked if we knew the man, sitting at the end of the table, who had told them of the death of Joseph Buquet. When we answered in the negative, they looked even more anxious. They took the keys from our hands, stared at them for a moment, and advised us to have new locks made. They said this in such a funny way that we began to laugh and to ask if there were thieves at the Opera. They replied that there was something worse—a ghost. We began to laugh again, feeling sure that this was a joke intended for our evening's entertainment.

Then, at their request, we became "serious," deciding to let them play their little game. They said that the ghost had given them orders. He wanted us to be pleasant to him and to honor any request he might make. Then they told us that the death of Joseph Buquet was a terrible reminder that, whenever they ignored the ghost's requests, disaster struck.

I looked at Richard. He was a man who loved a joke. He nodded his head sadly while the others spoke, and he looked like a man who regretted taking this job of manager. We both burst out laughing. Monsieur Debienne and Monsieur Poligny looked at us with expressions of amazement.

The joke became a little boring, and Richard asked half-seriously and half-jokingly, "But what does this ghost of yours want?"

Monsieur Poligny went to his desk and returned with a copy of the memorandum book, which contains the managers' rules for the Paris Opera. It looked exactly like the one we had except that at the end there was a passage in red ink and in a strange handwriting. This passage was as follows: "An allowance of 20,000 francs per month is to be made to the Opera ghost."

"Is that all? Doesn't he want anything else?" asked Monsieur Richard with great coolness.

"Yes, he does," replied Poligny. "Box Five will be for the use of the Opera ghost for every performance."

We rose from our chairs, shook their hands, and thanked them for the charming joke.

Monsieur Poligny asked, "Have you considered what the loss of Box Five meant to us? We did not sell it once. We really can't work to keep ghosts! We prefer to leave!"

Monsieur Richard said, "It seems to me that you were much too kind to the ghost. If I had such a trouble-making ghost, I would not hesitate to have him put in prison!"

"But how?" they cried together. "We have never seen him!"

"But when he comes to his box?"

"We have never seen him in his box."

"Then sell it."

"Sell the Opera ghost's box! Well, gentlemen, try it."

Then, we all four left the office. Richard and I had never laughed so much in our lives.

♦

Armand Moncharmin wrote so much and so often in his *Memories* that it is hard to believe he ever had time to do his job. He did not know a note of music, but he knew the right people. He was a journalist for a short time and enjoyed a large private income. He was a charming man and did not lack intelligence. As soon as he made up his mind to be a partner in the Opera, he chose the best possible manager and went straight to Firmin Richard.

Firmin Richard was a very famous and much respected writer of music who had a number of successful pieces in print. He had a strong personality, but unfortunately, he also had a very nasty temper.

In their first few days at the Opera, the new partners enjoyed the excitement of finding themselves at the head of such an admirable company. They had forgotten all about the crazy story of the ghost when something happened that proved to them that the joke—if it was a joke—was not over.

When Monsieur Richard entered his office, his secretary, Monsieur Rémy, showed him a letter which was marked "private." It was addressed in red ink, in handwriting he had seen before. He remembered the memorandum book and opened the letter:

Dear Mr. Manager:

I am sorry to bother you when you must be very busy. I know what you have done for Carlotta, Sorelli, and Jammes, and for a few others whose admirable qualities, of talent or genius, you have suspected.

When I use these words, I am not referring to La Carlotta, who sings like a child; nor to Sorelli, nor to little Jammes, who dances like a goat in a field. And I am not speaking of Christine Daaé either. Although her genius is certain, your jealousy prevents her from performing any important part. I am not happy that you have forbidden her to play the part of Margarita since her triumph the other evening, but I would like to hear her in the supporting role tonight.

I will ask you not to sell my box today nor on the following days, as I cannot end this letter without telling you how surprised I was to hear that my box had been sold on your orders. I did not protest, first, because I dislike unpleasant behavior, and second, because I thought that Monsieur Debienne and Monsieur Poligny had forgotten to tell you about me. But, I wrote to them and they replied that you knew all about my memorandum book and that you are treating me with complete disrespect. If you wish to live in peace, you must not take away my private box.

Your Most Obedient Servant,

Opera Ghost.

Monsieur Richard had just finished reading the letter when Monsieur Moncharmin entered, carrying one exactly the same. They looked at each other and burst out laughing.

"They like this joke," said Monsieur Richard, "but I don't call it funny."

"What does it all mean?" asked Monsieur Moncharmin. "Do they imagine that because they have been managers of the Opera, we are going to let them have a box for an indefinite period?"

"I am not in the mood to let myself be laughed at for long," said Monsieur Richard.

"It's harmless enough," observed Monsieur Moncharmin. "What is it they really want? A box for tonight?"

Monsieur Richard told his secretary to send tickets for Box Five to Monsieur Debienne and Monsieur Poligny, if it was not sold. It was not, and the tickets were sent off to them. The new managers regretted that two men of that age could amuse themselves with such childish tricks.

♦

The next morning, the managers received a card of thanks from the ghost:

Dear Mr. Manager:

Thanks. Charming evening. Daaé wonderful. Carlotta as usual. Will write you soon for my allowance of 20,000 francs.

Kind wishes,

O.G.

On the other hand, there was a letter from Monsieur Debienne and Monsieur Poligny:

Gentlemen:

    We are very grateful for your kind thoughts, but you will easily understand that we have no right to sit in Box Five, which is the property of the Opera ghost.

"Oh, those two are beginning to annoy me!" shouted Monsieur Richard.

And that evening Box Five was sold.

The next morning, Monsieur Richard and Monsieur Moncharmin found an inspector's report in their office. The report said that something had happened the night before, in Box Five. There were people making a lot of noise and annoying others. When the inspector went to the box, they did not seem to be in their right mind and they made stupid remarks. He warned them, but as soon as he left, they began laughing again. The other people in the opera house protested, so he called for a guard to throw them out.

"Send for the inspector," said Monsieur Richard to his secretary, Rémy. And when the secretary returned with the inspector, "Tell us what happened," he demanded.

"As soon as those people entered the box, they came out again and called the box-keeper. They said, 'Look in the box: there's no one there, is there?' 'No,' said the woman. 'Well,' they said, 'when we went in, we heard a voice saying *that the box was reserved*.'"

"However," shouted Monsieur Richard, "there was no one in the box, was there?"

"No one, sir! No one at all, sir, I swear!"

"And what did the box-keeper say?"

"Oh, she just said it was the Opera ghost!"

"Send for the box-keeper!" shouted Monsieur Richard to Rémy. His anger was boiling up inside him. "Who is this Opera ghost?" he demanded to know.

The inspector was desperate. He could not speak. He backed away.

"Have you ever seen . . . the Opera ghost?"

The inspector shook his head.

"I am going to find out what this is all about."

The scenery manager came in to discuss various matters of business with Monsieur Richard. The inspector thought he could go, so slowly and quietly he was moving toward the door, when Monsieur Richard nailed him to the floor with a thundering, "Stay where you are!"

Rémy returned with the box-keeper.

"What's your name?" asked Monsieur Richard.

"Madame* Giry. You know me well enough, sir; I'm the mother of little Giry, little Meg!"

Richard looked at Madame Giry, in her old coat, her worn shoes, and her old dress and dirty hat. He either did not know or could not remember meeting Madame Giry, nor little Giry. But Madame Giry's pride was so great that she imagined everybody knew her.

"Never heard of her!" the manager said. "Tell me, what happened last night?"

"I wanted to see you, sir, and talk to you about it, so that you wouldn't have the same unpleasantness as Monsieur Debienne and Monsieur Poligny."

"What happened last night?"

"I'll tell you what happened. The ghost was annoyed again!"

Monsieur Richard was getting very angry, so Monsieur Moncharmin continued the questioning. Madame Giry was not at all surprised that a voice had said that the box was being used although there was nobody in the box. Nobody could see the ghost, but everybody could hear him, she explained.

Monsieur Moncharmin interrupted her. "Have you spoken to the ghost, my good lady?"

* Madame: the French word for Mrs.

16

"As I am speaking to you now, sir!" she replied.

"And when the ghost speaks to you, what does he say?"

"Well, he tells me to bring him a footrest!"

This time, Richard burst out laughing.

"Instead of laughing, you'd be wise to do as Monsieur Poligny did. He found out for himself!" she said.

"Found out about what?" asked Moncharmin, who had never been so amused in all his life.

"About the ghost, of course! They were playing *La Juive*★ and Monsieur Poligny thought he would watch the performance from the ghost's box ... Well, when Leopold cries, 'Let us fly!', Monsieur Poligny got up and walked out quite stiffly ..."

"That doesn't tell us how the Opera ghost asked you for a footrest," said Moncharmin.

"Well, from that evening, no one tried to take the ghost's private box from him. The manager gave orders that he must have it at each performance. And, whenever he came, he asked me for a footrest."

"You say, 'he'?"

"Yes, he has a man's voice, a lovely man's voice. When he comes to the Opera, it's usually in the middle of the first act. He knocks gently three times on the door of Box Five. The first time this happened, I was surprised, but he said to me, 'Don't be frightened, Madame Giry, I'm the Opera ghost!'"

The two managers looked at the inspector, who put his fingers to his forehead to give his opinion that the widow was mad. Madame Giry told about the ghost's generosity—about the money and little presents he had left for her.

Finally, Monsieur Moncharmin said, "That's enough, Madame Giry. You can go." Then he told the inspector that they no longer needed that madwoman's services. When they were alone,

★ *La Juive*: an opera by Halévy.

the managers decided that they should inspect Box Five for themselves.

Chapter 3   The Angel of Music

Christine Daaé did not immediately continue her triumph at the Opera. After that famous night, she sang only once. It seemed that she was no longer in control of her life. I believe Christine Daaé was frightened by what had happened to her. I have a letter of hers from this period: "I don't know myself when I sing," wrote the poor child. The viscount, Raoul Chagny, tried unsuccessfully to see her. He wrote to her and desperately waited for her reply. When it came, he read:

> Monsieur:
>   I have not forgotten the little boy who went into the sea to rescue my scarf. I am going to Perros-Guirec, where my father is buried with his violin. You knew my father and he was very fond of you. I will go to the graveyard of the little church where we used to play as children. And where we said goodbye for the last time.

Viscount Chagny hurried to the train station. He read Christine's note again and again, and remembered the sweetest days of his childhood. He questioned the train driver and learned that a young lady who looked like a Parisian had gone to Perros-Guirec the day before and was staying at the Setting Sun. As he came nearer and nearer to her, he fondly remembered the story of the Angel of Music.

Christine Daaé's father was a poor Scandinavian farmer, and a talented violinist. His wife died when Christine was only six, so he sold his farm and went to Uppsala, the nearest town, in search of fortune. But he found only poverty.

He returned to the country, where he continued to play his

violin and his daughter sang. One day a music teacher, Monsieur Valérius, heard them and took them to Gothenburg. He thought that the father was the best violinist in the world, and the daughter had enormous talent. Valérius paid for her education and she made rapid progress. She was charming, pretty, and eager to please. When Monsieur Valérius and his wife moved to France, they took Daaé and Christine with them. Madame Valérius treated Christine as a daughter.

One summer, Daaé took Christine to Perros-Guirec, in a faraway corner of Brittany, for a week. He played his violin and she sang in the small towns. They slept at night in farm buildings and they would not take any money for their music. People could not understand the behavior of this farmer with his pretty child who sang like an angel from Heaven. But they followed them from village to village.

One day, a little boy was out for a walk on a stretch of golden beach. He followed the little girl whose pure, sweet voice seemed to capture him. There was a high wind which blew Christine's scarf out to sea. She cried out, but the scarf was already far away on the waves. Then she heard a voice say: "It's all right, I'll go and get your scarf out of the sea."

And she saw a little boy running fast. He brought it back and Christine laughed and kissed him. That boy was Raoul Chagny, who was staying at Lannion with his aunt.

That week, they played together every day. One day Christine's father, who often told them stories, told them one that began: "Little Lotte thought of everything and nothing. She loved her toys, her little red shoes, and her violin. But most of all, she loved to hear the Angel of Music when she went to sleep."

The Angel of Music was in all of Daddy Daaé's stories. He always said that every great musician received a visit from the Angel at least once in his life. If the Angel visits a small baby, that

19

child grows up to play the violin at the age of six better than men of fifty. This is what happened to little Lotte.

No one ever sees the Angel, but he is heard by those who are meant to hear him. He often comes when they least expect him. Then they hear heavenly music, and a divine voice that they remember all their lives. People who are visited by the Angel cannot touch an instrument, or open their mouths to sing, without producing sounds that put all other human sounds to shame. Then people who do not know that the Angel has visited those people say that they have genius.

Little Christine asked her father if he had heard the Angel of Music. But Daddy Daaé shook his head sadly. Then his eyes lit up and he said, "You will hear him one day, my child! When I am in Heaven, I will send him to you!"

Three years later, Raoul and Christine met again at Perros-Guirec. Monsieur Valérius was dead, but his widow remained in France with Daaé and his daughter. The young man, Raoul, had come to Perros, hoping to find them, and went straight to the house where they used to stay.

Christine turned red when she saw Raoul. They talked shyly until evening, telling each other things, but not their true feelings. When Raoul left, he kissed Christine's trembling hand and said, "Mademoiselle, I will never forget you!" He went away regretting his words because he knew that a poor girl like Christine could never be the wife of a viscount.

Her father died, and suddenly she seemed to have lost, with him, her voice, her soul, and her genius. She continued to live with Madame Valérius and went to a very fine music school.

The first time Raoul saw Christine at the Opera, he was struck by her beauty and the memories it brought back. He followed her, but she did not see him. He suffered because she was very beautiful and he was shy and dared not admit his love, not even to himself. Then came the lightning flash of that performance:

an angel's voice was heard on earth—and it captured his heart.

And then . . . and then there was that man's voice behind the door—"You must love me!"—but no one in the room . . .

Why did she laugh when he reminded her of the scarf? Why didn't she recognize him? And why had she written to him?

At last he reached Perros. Raoul walked into the smoky sitting room of the Setting Sun and at once saw Christine, smiling and showing no surprise.

"So you have come," she said. "I knew I would find you here when I came back from church because someone told me you had come."

"Who?" asked Raoul, taking her little hand in his.

"My poor father, who is dead."

Then Raoul asked, "Did your father tell you that I love you, Christine, and that I cannot live without you?"

Christine's face was red. In a trembling voice, she said, "Me? You're dreaming, my friend!"

And she burst out laughing to hide her feelings.

"Don't laugh, Christine; I am quite serious," Raoul answered.

And she replied seriously, "I did not make you come to tell me things like that."

"You made me come, Christine. You knew that I would hurry to Perros. How could you send that letter, if you did not think I loved you?"

"I don't know what I thought. Maybe I was wrong to write to you. Your sudden appearance in my dressing room the other evening reminded me of the time long past . . ."

Raoul noticed that Christine was upset. He asked her why she had laughed when he reminded her of the scarf and why she had pretended that she did not know him. Raoul was surprised at the roughness of his questions, when he had wanted to speak words of gentleness and love. But he could see no way out except to behave unpleasantly.

"You don't answer!" he said angrily and unhappily. "Well, I will answer for you. It was because there was someone in the room, Christine. Someone who you did not wish to know that you could be interested in anyone else!"

"What are you saying? Who are you referring to?"

"To the man you spoke to and said, 'I sing only for you! Tonight I gave you my soul and I am dead!'"

"Then you were listening behind the door?"

"Yes, because I love you . . . And I heard everything . . ."

"You heard what?" she asked, becoming strangely calm.

"He said to you, 'Christine, you must love me!'"

Suddenly, she looked very unwell. Raoul rushed to catch her before she fainted, but she quickly recovered.

"Tell me all that you heard," she said.

"I heard him say, 'Your soul is a beautiful thing, child, and I thank you. No king ever received such a fair gift. The angels in Heaven cried tonight.'"

Christine's hand covered her heart and her eyes stared ahead like a madwoman's. Raoul was struck with terror.

"Christine!" The young man tried to take her in his arms, but she escaped and ran away.

Raoul did not know what to do. The hours that he had hoped to spend with the young girl slipped past. She stayed in her room and would not dine with him. Later that evening, he went to the graveyard, then climbed the hill and sat down. He looked out over the sea, and was surrounded by icy darkness, but he did not feel the cold. Hearing a noise, he turned and saw Christine coming toward him!

"Raoul, I have decided to tell you something very serious . . . Do you remember the story of the Angel of Music?"

"Of course, I do," he said. "I believe your father first told it to us here."

"And here he said, 'When I am in Heaven, my child, I will

send him to you.' Well, Raoul, my father is in Heaven and I have been visited by the Angel of Music. He comes to my dressing room to give me lessons daily."

"In your dressing room?" he repeated.

"Yes, that is where you heard him."

"I? I heard the Angel of Music?"

"*He* was the one who was talking when you were listening behind the door. But I thought I was the only one to hear his voice. Imagine how surprised I was this morning when you told me that you could hear him, too."

Raoul burst out laughing, which made Christine very angry. She said, "If you had opened the door, you would have seen that there was nobody in the room!"

"That's true! I did open the door, when you were gone, and I found no one in the room."

"Well?"

The viscount answered, "Well, Christine, I think that somebody is making fun of you."

She cried out angrily and ran away. He ran after her, but she shouted, "Leave me! Leave me!" and she disappeared.

Raoul returned to the Setting Sun, feeling very sad and tired. Christine had gone to her room and would not speak to him. He went to bed and tried to sleep. There was no sound from Christine's room.

However, about eleven-thirty, he heard her leave her room, and he heard her speaking to someone downstairs. He looked out of the window and watched her leave. He climbed down the tree outside his bedroom window and went after her.

The next morning he was brought back, more dead than alive. He had been found stretched out on the steps of the little church. The owner of the Setting Sun took him in and immediately ran for Christine. They did their best to help him and he soon opened his eyes. When he saw his friend's charming face, he recovered quickly.

A few weeks later, after the tragedy at the Opera, which you will soon know about, the police spoke to Viscount Chagny about that night at Perros-Guirec. He told them that he had followed Christine to the church, where she knelt down at her father's grave and began to pray. At midnight, Mademoiselle Daaé lifted her eyes to the sky and stretched out her arms. Suddenly, Raoul heard the most perfect music. It was a piece of music that Monsieur Daaé used to play to them when they were children—*The Resurrection of Lazarus*.* Christine stood up and walked to the gate, but she did not see or hear Raoul. When Raoul got up to leave, a skull rolled toward him . . . then another . . . and another. There were hundreds of them up against the wall of the church, held in position by a wire. He had seen these skulls when he had been at the church earlier that day, as they are often seen in old Breton churches. Then he saw a shadow move along the church wall. He ran up. The shadow pushed open the door and entered the church. Raoul caught his coat. The shadow turned around and Raoul saw . . . the face of Death with a pair of burnt-out eyes. He told the police that he felt he had been face-to-face with the devil. Then he fainted, and he saw nothing again until he was in the Setting Sun.

◆

At the opera house, Monsieur Richard and Monsieur Moncharmin went to have a look at Box Five. They stood below and looked up. It was dark in the theater, but both men saw a shape in the box. At that moment, they seized each other's hand. They stood, wide-eyed, but the shape had disappeared. They went out and spoke about what they had seen. Moncharmin had seen a face of Death resting on the edge of the box. Richard had seen the shape of an old woman who looked like Madame Giry.

---

* *The Resurrection of Lazarus*: a piece of music about a man who comes back to life after death.

They both ran to Box Five, laughing like madmen, went inside, and found no shape at all. They looked under the furniture in the box, but found nothing. There was nothing different about this box.

"Those people are making fools of us!" said Monsieur Richard. "On Saturday, let's both see the performance from Box Five!"

Chapter 4   The Curse

On the Saturday morning, the managers found a letter from O.G.:

My Dear Managers:
So it is to be war between us?
If you still care for peace, here are my four conditions:
1. You must give me back my private box for my use only.
2. The part of Margarita will be sung this evening by Christine Daaé—not Carlotta, who will be sick.
3. I must have the loyal services of Madame Giry, my box-keeper, and you will give her back her job immediately.
4. Reply by letter through Madame Giry, who will make sure that it reaches me, saying that you accept the conditions in my memorandum book and will pay my allowance. I will inform you later how you will give it to me.
If you refuse, you will perform *Faust* tonight in a house with a curse on it.

O.G.

At that moment the door opened. It was Madame Giry, holding a letter in her hand.

"Excuse me, gentlemen, but I had a letter this morning, from the Opera ghost. He told me to come to you, that you had something to . . ."

She was unable to complete her sentence because she saw

Monsieur Richard's face, which was a terrible sight. He seized her, spun her around, and kicked her out—leaving a footprint on the back of her skirt. The Opera rang with her screams and violent protests as she threatened him.

About the same time, Carlotta, who lived in a small house on Rue du Faubourg St. Honoré,★ was brought her letters. There was one written in red ink which said:

> If you appear tonight, you must be prepared for a great misfortune at the moment when you open your mouth to sing— a misfortune worse than death.

She had never received a letter as threatening as this, and she thought there was a plot against her, but she was not going to be frightened.

In fact, if there was a plot, it was led by Carlotta herself against poor Christine, who did not suspect it at all. Carlotta had never forgiven Christine for the triumph she achieved when she took Carlotta's place. After that night, Carlotta never missed a performance and asked her powerful friends to persuade the managers not to give Christine an opportunity for a fresh triumph. Now, she collected all of her supporters and told them that Christine Daaé was threatening her. She asked them to fill the house that night with her, Carlotta's, admirers.

Monsieur Richard's secretary called to ask about her health. She replied that she was well, but that "even if she were dying," she would sing the part of Margarita that evening.

It was five o'clock when the mail brought a second letter in red ink. It was short and simple:

> You have a bad cold. If you are wise, you will see that it is madness to try to sing tonight.

★ Rue de Faubourg St. Honoré: a famous street in Paris. Rue is the French word for street.

Carlotta was not afraid; her friends were all at the Opera that night and they were looking around for the enemy. The only unusual thing was the presence of Monsieur Richard and Monsieur Moncharmin in Box Five.

Monsieur Richard, who was sitting in the ghost's own chair, asked Moncharmin, "Well, has the ghost whispered a word in your ear yet?"

"Wait, don't be in such a hurry," replied Moncharmin. "The performance has only just begun and you know that the ghost does not usually come until the middle of the first act."

Nothing happened during the first act, but this did not surprise Carlotta's friends because Margarita does not sing in this act. The managers looked at each other when the curtain came down.

"That's one!" said Moncharmin.

"Yes, the ghost is late," said Richard.

"It's not a bad performance," said Moncharmin, "for an opera house with a curse on it."

Richard smiled and pointed to a fat woman in a bright dress, sitting between two men who were wearing cheap coats.

"Who are they?" asked Moncharmin.

"They are my servant, her husband, and her brother."

"Did you give them their tickets?"

"I did . . . My servant has never been to the Opera before and, as she is now going to come every night, I wanted her to have a good seat. After tonight, she will be showing other people to theirs." Monsieur Richard explained that he wanted his servant to have Madame Giry's job. Maybe then there would be no surprises in Box Five.

Then Christine Daaé came on stage as Siebel, looking charming in her boy's clothes. When Margarita crossed the stage and sang her only two lines for this second act, Carlotta was received enthusiastically by the audience. But nothing else happened.

The managers stepped out at the end of the second act, and when they returned they found a box of candy on the little shelf. Who had put it there? They asked the box-keepers, but none of them knew. They returned and found a pair of opera glasses. Everything that Madame Giry had told them returned to their memory . . . and then . . . they seemed to feel some strangely cold air around them . . . They sat down in silence.

As Christine began to sing, she saw Viscount Chagny sitting next to his brother, and from that moment, her voice seemed less sure, less clear. The viscount put his head in his hands. The count, beside him, was upset because after Raoul had returned from Perros, the count had asked Christine Daaé for an appointment, but she refused to see him. He had wanted to speak to her about Raoul, and was very annoyed with her.

Raoul thought only of the letter he had received from Christine after that night in Perros. She told him that he must not try to see her again. She said that she would never forget him and if he loved her, he would do what she asked. Their lives depended on it.

Carlotta entered. The audience clapped loudly. She sang with all her heart and soul, when suddenly . . . a terrible thing happened. Faust sang to her and Margarita replied, but not in her beautiful voice, but with the voice of a toad: "Co-ack!" There was a look of confusion on Carlotta's face and on the faces of the audience. This was a disaster!

During these few moments, in Box Five, Monsieur Moncharmin and Monsieur Richard turned very pale. They had felt the breath of the ghost. Moncharmin's hair stood on end. Richard wiped his forehead. Yes, the ghost was there, around them, behind them, beside them; they felt his presence without seeing him. They heard his breath, close, close, close to them! They trembled. They thought of running away . . . They dared not . . . They dared not make a move or exchange a word. The ghost would know that they knew he was there! What was going to happen?

This happened: "*Co-ack!*"

Their scream of horror was heard all over the house. They looked at Carlotta, but they did not seem to recognize her. That girl was giving a signal for some greater disaster! Now they understood. The ghost had warned them. The house had a curse on it! Richard called to Carlotta, "Well, go on!"

She began to sing ... then ... the toad started again! "*Co-ack! Co-ack!*"

The managers fell back in their chairs. The ghost was laughing quietly behind their backs! And, at last, they heard his voice in their ears, the impossible voice, the mouthless voice: "*She is singing tonight to bring the chandelier down!*"

They both looked up and made a terrible cry. The chandelier was coming down! It crashed! Shouts of terror rang out and there was a wild rush for the doors.

The next day, the newspapers told the story. The chandelier had crashed on the head of the poor woman who had come to the Opera for the first time in her life, the one who had been given Madame Giry's job of box-keeper. She died on the spot. One newspaper wrote:

TWO HUNDRED KILOS
ON THE HEAD OF A SERVANT

♦

That tragic evening was bad for everybody. Carlotta was very unwell afterward. Christine Daaé disappeared after the performance and was not seen by anyone for two weeks. Raoul was seriously worried at never seeing her name on the program; *Faust* was played without her.

Raoul went to the managers' office to ask why Christine had disappeared, and he found them both looking extremely worried. They would not speak about the fall of the chandelier, but they were, at least partly, responsible. It had been decided that the cause of death of the servant was accidental, but that the old and new managers were responsible for not noticing that the chandelier needed repairs.

The managers became impatient with everyone, except Madame Giry—who had her job back. They were impatient with the viscount when he asked about Christine. They told him that she was away for an unlimited period, for reasons of health.

The viscount decided to visit Madame Valérius. She was sick in bed but agreed to see him.

"Monsieur Chagny!" she cried happily. "It's Heaven that sends you here! We can talk of *her*!"

"Madame . . . where is Christine?"

"She is with her good genius!" the old woman answered calmly. "With the Angel of Music!" Then, putting her finger to her lips, she warned him, "You must not tell anyone! I'm very fond of you, Monsieur Raoul . . . And Christine is, too!"

"What makes you think that?" he asked in a low voice.

"She used to speak about you every day. She told me that you had asked her to marry you." The old lady began to laugh.

Raoul jumped up from his chair, embarrassed and suffering great tortures.

"Where are you going? Do you think I will let you go like that?" she asked. "I'm sorry for laughing, but didn't you know? Did you think that Christine was free?"

"Is she going to marry someone?" he asked, trying to control his emotions.

"No! But you know as well as I do that Christine couldn't marry, even if she wanted to!"

"But I don't know anything about it! Why can't she?"

"Because the Angel of Music forbids her to! He tells her that if she got married, she would never hear him again. That's all!

And that he would go away forever! So, you understand, she can't let the Angel of Music go."

"Yes, yes," Raoul answered, understanding nothing.

"I thought she told you all this in Perros. He arranged to meet her there at Daaé's grave, and he promised to play her *The Resurrection of Lazarus* on her father's violin."

"Madame, will you kindly tell me where that genius lives?"

"In Heaven!"

This simple old woman's answer surprised him. He did not know what to say. He now realized the possible state of mind of a girl brought up by a superstitious Scandinavian violinist and a superstitious old woman. The thought of this made him feel uncomfortable.

"How long has she known this genius?"

"About three months . . . yes, three months ago he started giving her lessons."

"The genius gives her lessons? Where?"

"In her dressing room. In the Opera at eight o'clock in the morning, when there is no one around!"

Raoul quickly left and went to his brother's house. "What a fool I have been!" he thought. "How cruel she is!"

His brother was waiting for him and Raoul fell into his arms like a child. Of course, Raoul could not tell him the story of the Angel of Music—Philippe would think Christine was mad.

Philippe told Raoul, "Christine was seen last night in a carriage, with a man, in the woods."

At first, Raoul refused to believe this. But his brother told him all the details. She had been seen riding in a carriage, with the window down. The moon was shining brightly. The man's shadowy figure was leaning back in the dark and the carriage went no faster than a man walking.

That evening, Raoul went out with the count for dinner, but left early. He found himself by ten o'clock in the woods where

Christine had been seen. It was bitterly cold, and there was no one on the road, which was brightly lit from the moon. He waited. After half an hour, a carriage turned the corner and came quietly and slowly in his direction.

"Christine!" Her name burst out of him. It was a great mistake because it caused the carriage to suddenly fly past him at great speed. Someone quickly closed the window and her face disappeared. She had passed without answering his cry.

In the morning, his servant found him sitting on his bed. He had not undressed. When he saw Raoul's face, the servant thought that a disaster had happened. Raoul quickly took his letters from the servant's hand. He recognized Christine's paper and handwriting. She had written:

Dear:

Go to the masked party at the Opera on the night after tomorrow. At midnight, be in the little room behind the stairs. Stand near the door that leads to the great hall. Don't mention this appointment to anyone on earth. Wear a white mask and a white coat. If you love me, do not let yourself be recognized.

Christine.

Chapter 5   A Party Mask

The letter was covered with mud and written on it was *To be handed to Viscount Chagny*. Did she throw it from the carriage, hoping that someone would find it and deliver it? That is, in fact, what happened.

Raoul read it again and again. Whose prisoner was she? What evil person had carried her away . . . and how? And now he was taking her for drives in the woods. Raoul pitied her—and he cursed her. But, he bought a white mask.

He climbed the grand stairs at five minutes to twelve, and entered the room mentioned in Christine's letter. He found it full of people—those going for supper passing those who were returning from taking a glass of wine.

He did not have to wait long. Someone in a black mask and a black coat gave a quick squeeze to the tips of his fingers. He understood that it was Christine and followed her.

"Is that you, Christine?" he asked, between his teeth.

She raised her fingers to her lips, warning him not to mention her name again.

He was afraid of losing her, after meeting her again in such strange circumstances. His feelings of anger were gone. He was ready to forgive her. He was in love. As he followed his guide, he noticed a group crowding around a person whose mask, strange manner, and terrible appearance were causing great excitement. It was a man dressed all in red, with a large hat and feathers on top of a wonderful mask of death. He wore a long red coat with gold letters that read: *Don't touch me! I am Red Death!*

As Raoul passed by, he nearly cried out, "The face of Death from Perros-Guirec!" He had recognized him, but Christine took him by the arm and led him away. They went up two floors, where she took him to the back of a private box and told him not to show himself. Raoul took off his mask; Christine kept hers on.

She stopped and listened, then said, "He's gone up higher . . . Oh, no! He's coming down again!"

Raoul saw a red foot followed by another . . . then the whole red coat of Red Death met his eyes. And again he saw the face of Death that he had seen in Perros-Guirec. Just as Raoul started to rush out, Christine closed the door. Raoul tried to push her but, with surprising strength, she stopped him.

"He will not escape!" said Raoul.

"Who? Who will not?" she asked in a changed voice.

"The evil genius of the churchyard at Perros! Red Death! Your Angel of Music! I will take off his mask and see who you love and who loves you!"

He burst into a mad laugh. Christine stretched out her arms across the door to prevent him from opening it.

"In the name of our love, Raoul, you will not pass!"

He stopped. What had she said? In the name of their love? She had never admitted before that she loved him. But she had had enough opportunities. She was trying to gain a few seconds! She wanted to give Red Death time to escape!

With childish hatred, Raoul said, "You are lying! You do not love me and you have never loved me! What a poor fool I must be! Why did you give me every reason for hope, at Perros? I am an honest man and I believed that you were an honest woman, but your only intention was to deceive me. And you go around this party with Red Death! I hate you!"

And he burst into tears. She allowed him to insult her. She thought of only one thing, to stop him leaving the box. "You will ask me for forgiveness one day, for all those ugly words, Raoul. And when you do, I will forgive you!"

He shook his head. "No, no, you have driven me mad! I had only one hope—to give my name to a poor orphan!"

"Raoul! How can you say that to me?"

"I will die of shame!"

"No, dear, live!" said Christine's changed voice. "Goodbye, Raoul."

"You must let me come and clap for you from time to time," he said angrily.

"I will never sing again, Raoul! You will never see me again!"

"What darkness are you returning to? What Heaven or what Hell?"

"I came to tell you, dear, but I can't tell you now... you would not believe me. It is finished."

She spoke so desperately that he began to feel regret for his cruelty. "Anyone would be deceived by all of this. Explain yourself, Christine," he said.

Christine simply took off her mask and said, "Dear, it is a tragedy!"

"My dearest, my dearest!" he cried when he saw her face. It brought both surprise and terror to his heart. The shadows under her eyes! The gray skin! The lines! "You promised to forgive me!"

"Maybe . . . maybe one day," she said as she put her mask on and left, forbidding him to follow. He dared not try to follow her, but watched her until she was out of sight.

Raoul went to look for Red Death, but could not find him. At two o'clock, he went to Christine's dressing room and knocked gently on the door, but there was no answer. He went inside and hid in the inner room, which was separated from the dressing room by a curtain.

Christine entered, took off her mask, and threw it on the table. She let her pretty head fall into her two hands. What was she thinking of? Raoul heard her softly say, "Poor Erik!" Who was this Erik? And why was Christine pitying Erik when Raoul was so unhappy? She wrote something on a piece of paper, but she seemed to be listening. Raoul also listened. Where did that strange sound come from? A faint singing seemed to come from the walls.

Raoul could now hear the words. He heard a man's voice, a beautiful soft voice coming nearer and nearer . . . through the wall. Christine rose and spoke to the voice. "Here I am, Erik. I am ready. But you are late."

Raoul looked out from behind the curtain, but could not believe his eyes. Christine's face lit up with a beautiful smile. The voice was singing *The Wedding Night Song*. Raoul pulled back the curtain. Christine was moving to the back of the room, where one whole wall was a great mirror. He could see Christine in the mirror, but not himself, as he was behind her.

The singer continued. Christine continued walking toward the mirror. Raoul reached out to the "two" Christines—the real one and the one in the mirror. But he was suddenly thrown back when an icy wind swept over his face. He saw not two, but four, eight, twenty Christines spinning around him, laughing at him and escaping so quickly that he could not touch one of them.

He rushed up to the mirror. He struck at the walls. Nobody! And the voice continued singing, "*Our lives are joined for ever and a day!*"

Raoul sat down and let his head fall into his hands. When he raised it, tears ran down his cheeks—tears common to all the lovers on earth. "Who is this Erik?" he asked.

♦

The next day, when Raoul went to visit Madame Valérius, to his great surprise he found Christine sitting next to the old woman, who was sleeping. He noticed a plain gold ring on Christine's finger. When he asked her about it, she answered that it was a present. Raoul, his heart breaking, asked to whom she had promised herself. But Christine refused to give any information.

Then, Raoul told her what he had seen and heard the previous night. When he told her that he knew the Angel of Music was called Erik, she turned as white as a sheet.

"Oh, unhappy man! Do you want to be killed?" she asked.

Raoul answered, "Maybe" with so much desperate love that Christine could not hold back her tears. She took his hands in hers and said, "Raoul, you must never try to understand the mystery of the man's voice."

"Is the mystery so terrible?"

"There is no more awful mystery on this earth. Swear to me

that you will make no attempt to find out, and that you will never come to my dressing room unless I send for you."

"Then promise to send for me sometimes, Christine."

"I promise."

"When?"

"Tomorrow."

"Then I swear to do as you ask." He kissed her hands and went away, cursing Erik and promising himself to be patient.

Chapter 6 Tragedy

The next day, when Raoul saw Christine at the Opera, she was still wearing the plain gold ring. She was gentle and kind to him, and she talked to him about the plans which he was forming, of his future, of his career.

He told her that the date of his journey to the North Pole had been put forward and that he would leave France in three or four weeks. She wanted him to look forward to this journey, but without her love to take with him he found little joy in these plans.

Then, Christine had an idea, an idea that filled her with great happiness. "We will have these three or four weeks to pretend . . . to pretend that we have plans to marry when you return. This is a happiness that can harm no one!"

Raoul liked the idea. He took her hand and said, "Mademoiselle, I have the honor to ask you to marry me."

"Oh, Raoul, how happy we will be! We will play at this all day long!"

Every afternoon for the next week, they met in the singer's dressing room and amused themselves by dining on three cookies and two glasses of wine. They made promises to each other, as children do when they play. But then, at the end of that first week, Raoul stopped playing and said, "I will not go to the North Pole!"

Christine suddenly discovered the danger of the game and disappeared for two days. When she returned, she had good news. Carlotta had not been able to appear on the stage since that night of the terrible "*Co-ack!*" and now Christine had been offered her place.

Raoul went to listen to her. It was a new triumph for Christine, but for Raoul it was hell. A voice whispered in his ear, "She is wearing the ring again tonight; and you did not give it to her. She gave her soul again tonight, and did not give it to you. If she will not tell you what she has been doing the past two days . . . you must go and ask Erik!"

He ran backstage after the performance and threw himself on his knees in front of her. He swore to her that he would go to the North Pole, but that she must never again take from him one hour of the happiness she had promised. She cried. They kissed.

Suddenly, she moved away from him and listened at the door. Then, in a low voice, she whispered, "Be happy, Raoul. I sang for you tonight!"

Their time together over the next weeks was spent going for walks—not outdoors in the fresh air, but inside the Opera with its seventeen floors. Once, when they were passing a trap door, Raoul stopped over the dark hole and said, "You have shown me all over the upper part of your opera house, Christine, but there are strange stories about the lower part. Shall we go down?"

In a trembling voice she whispered, "Never! . . . I will not let you go there! Besides, it's not mine. *Everything that is underground belongs to him!*"

"So he lives down there, does he?" Raoul said angrily.

"I never said so. Come away!"

She tried to pull him away, but he was attracted to the dark hole. Suddenly, the trap door closed, and so quickly that they did not see the hand that closed it. They stared in silence.

"Maybe *he* was there," Raoul said, at last.

"No, no, it was the trap door shutters. They must do something, you know, so they open and close the doors for no reason."

"But suppose it was *he*, Christine!"

"No, no, he has shut himself up; he's working."

"What is he working at?"

"Oh, something terrible! But it's better for us . . . when he's working at that, he sees nothing; he does not eat, drink, or breathe for many days and nights . . . he has no time to amuse himself with trap doors."

"Are you afraid of him?" Raoul asked.

"No, no, of course not," she said. But for some days after that, she avoided the trap doors.

One afternoon she arrived late, her face desperately pale and her eyes desperately red.

"I will remove you from his power, Christine, I swear it. And you will not think of him again."

"Is it possible?" she asked, allowing herself this doubt, this encouragement, as she dragged the young man up to the top floor of the theater—far, very far, from the trap doors.

"Higher!" she kept saying.

They were soon under the roof. And despite the care that she took to look behind her at every moment, she failed to see a shadow which followed her like her own shadow. It stopped when she stopped, started when she started. Raoul saw nothing either because when he had Christine in front of him, nothing interested him that happened behind.

They reached the roof. It was a beautiful spring evening.

"Soon we will go farther and faster than the clouds, to the end of the world, and then you will leave me, Raoul. But if, when the moment comes for you to take me away, I refuse to go with you—well, you must carry me off by force!"

"Are you afraid that you will change your mind, Christine?"

"I don't know. He is a devil!" she said, as she sat wrapped in his arms. "I am afraid now of going back to live with him!"

"What makes you go back, Christine?"

"If I do not go back, terrible misfortunes may happen! But I can't do it! I can't! I know one ought to be sorry for people who live underground . . . But he is too terrible! I have only one day left; and if I do not go, he will come and get me with his voice. And he will drag me with him, underground, and go on his knees in front of me, with his face of Death! And he will tell me that he loves me! And he will cry! Oh, those tears, Raoul, those tears in those two black holes. I cannot see those tears again!"

Raoul pressed her to his heart.

"Let us escape at once, Christine!"

He tried to drag her away, but she stopped him.

"No, not now. That would be too cruel. Let him hear me sing tomorrow evening . . . and then we will go away. Come and get me from my dressing room at midnight exactly! He will be waiting for me in the dining room by the lake. We will be free and you will take me away! You must promise me that, Raoul, even if I refuse. I feel that, if I go back this time, I may never return." She stopped for a minute, then said, "Did you hear something?"

"No, I heard nothing," said Raoul.

"It's terrible to be always trembling like this! But up here we are in no danger. We are at home, in the sky, in the open air, in the light. I have never seen *him* by daylight . . . it must be awful! Oh, the first time I saw him! I thought that he was going to die!"

"Why?" asked Raoul, frightened by her strange words.

"Because I had seen him!"

Suddenly, both Raoul and Christine turned around.

"Someone is in pain," said Raoul. "Maybe someone has been hurt. Did you hear?"

"I don't know. Even when he is not there, my ears are full of his sounds. Still, if you heard . . ."

They stood up and looked around. There was no one. They sat down again and Raoul said, "Tell me how you saw him first."

"I had heard him for three months without seeing him. The first time I thought, as you did, that the divine voice was singing in another room. I looked everywhere, but I could not find the voice. And it not only sang, but it spoke to me and answered my questions, like a real man's voice. But it was as beautiful as the voice of an angel. I had never been visited by the Angel of Music whom my father had promised to send me. I asked him if he was the Angel of Music, and he replied that he was. From that time, the voice and I became great friends, and he gave me lessons. In a few weeks' time, I hardly knew myself when I sang. The voice said, 'Wait and see; we will surprise Paris!' Then I saw you for the first time one evening, in the Opera. I was so glad and I did not think about hiding my feelings when I reached my dressing room. The voice noticed. I told him about you and my feelings for you. Then the voice was silent. I called to him, but he did not reply. I was afraid that he had gone forever. That night I told Madame Valérius and she said, 'Well of course, the voice is jealous!' And that, dear, made me realize that I love you."

Neither Christine nor Raoul noticed the shadow approaching them. Christine continued to tell Raoul her story. She told him that the voice wanted to possess her and that if she gave her love to a human, he would go back to Heaven. She did not want to lose the Angel of Music who was sent by her dear father. She told Raoul that the voice was jealous and that was why she pretended not to know Raoul when she opened her eyes and saw him in her dressing room. Then, she decided to go to Perros to pray on her father's grave, and she told the voice that she was going to ask Raoul to go, too, because she was annoyed with the voice's arguments with her about Raoul.

She told Raoul that after the chandelier came down, she was so happy that he was unhurt—she could see Raoul with his brother—but she was afraid for the voice. Then, in her dressing room, his voice came to her and commanded her to come. She explained that her room seemed to become longer and the mirrors made such a strange effect that before she knew it, she was outside the room.

"I cried out," she told Raoul. "A stone-cold hand seized my wrist and did not let go. I was in the hands of a man in a large coat and wearing a mask that hid his whole face. My mouth opened to scream, but a hand closed it . . . a hand that smelled of death. Then I fainted."

She told Raoul that when she opened her eyes, she was being carried through the underground cellars of the opera house. She was taken through dark passages to the edge of a lake. In the blue light, she could see a boat. The man took her in the boat across the lake to a great room filled with flowers and said, "Don't be afraid, Christine; you are in no danger." It was the voice! Until that moment, she had not imagined that the voice and the Opera ghost were the same.

"My anger equaled my amazement," she told Raoul. "I rushed at the mask and tried to pull it off. The man said, 'You are in no danger if you do not touch the mask.' He forced me into a chair. The adventure was extraordinary, but at least I was not in the cellars of the Opera. I was, however, with a very strange and mysterious man who had succeeded in making those cellars his home—under the opera house, five floors below the level of the ground. I began to cry and the man understood my tears because he said, 'It is true, Christine! I am not the Angel of Music, nor a genius, nor a ghost . . . I am Erik!' "

"Christine," Raoul interrupted, "we are wrong to wait until tomorrow evening; we should go immediately."

"If he does not hear me sing tomorrow, it will cause him unbearable pain . . . and we risk being killed."

"Does he love you so much?"

"He would commit murder for me."

"Why did you go back to him?"

"Because I had to. And you will understand when I tell you how I left him."

"Oh, I hate him!" cried Raoul. "And you, Christine, do you hate him, too?"

"No," said Christine simply.

Raoul, in his confused emotional condition, accused Christine of loving Erik, a man who lived in an underground palace. She warned him that if she went back there, she would never return. Then, they sat in silence—the three of them: the two who spoke and the shadow that listened, behind them.

"Since you do not hate him, what feeling does he fill you with?" asked Raoul after some minutes.

"Horror!" she said. "He fills me with horror, but I do not hate him. He loves me! He has an enormous and tragic love for me! And when I told him that I could only hate him if he did not give me my freedom, . . . he offered it . . . he offered to show me the mysterious road. But then he sang and I was reminded that he was still the voice.

"The next day, he showed me his room, where he is writing a piece of music called *Don Juan Triumphant*★ which he began twenty years ago. And when I asked him to play some of it for me, he said, 'You must never ask me that. Some music is so terrible that it destroys all who approach it.' Then he suggested that we sing something from the Opera, but he said this in

★ Don Juan: the name for a man who is a great lover of women.

such a way that it was insulting to me, and he intended this."

"What did you do?" Raoul asked.

"We began singing and I sang with great sadness and terror, which I had never done before. Suddenly, I needed to see what face was under that mask, the face of the voice, and I tore off the mask. Oh, horror, horror, horror!"

A far-away voice sadly repeated, "Horror! Horror! Horror!" But the words were not clearly heard by the two lovers.

"If I live to be one hundred, I will always remember the cry of pain and anger which he made when the terrible sight appeared in front of my eyes. The face of Death that you saw at Perros and at the masked party was a *silent* horror, not alive. But imagine, the four black holes of Red Death's mask suddenly coming to life to express the extreme anger of a devil.

"I fell to my knees and he cursed and shouted, 'Look! You want to see me! Look at Erik's face! Now you know the face of the voice! I'm a very good-looking man, aren't I? When a woman has seen me, as you have, she belongs to me! She loves me forever! I am Don Juan triumphant!' And when I turned my head away, he angrily took my head with his dead fingers and twisted them into my hair."

"Enough! I will kill him! Tell me where the dining room on the lake is and I will kill him!" shouted Raoul.

"Listen, Raoul, he dragged me by my hair and then . . . and then . . . Oh, it's too terrible!"

"What?" Raoul asked, his voice full of suffering and anger.

"He seized my hands and dug them into his awful face. He tore his flesh with my nails. He was shouting, 'Maybe you think that I have another mask. Tear it off!' And then he said, 'I am built of death from head to foot, and this is a dead man who loves you and will never, never leave you! You can never leave me again. While you thought that maybe I was handsome, you could go because I knew you would return . . . but now you know my ugliness. Now you would run away and never come back. So I will keep you here! Why did you want to see me, Christine? My own father never saw me and my mother—in order not to see me—gave me my first mask!'

"He let go of me and cried, a terrible cry of great pain and sadness. Then he went to his room and closed the door. I heard him play his *Don Juan Triumphant* and it was both awful and wonderful. It expressed every emotion, every suffering known to man. I opened the door and he rose. 'Erik,' I cried, 'show me your face without fear. You are the most unhappy and the most heavenly of men—a great genius.' He fell at my feet. He kissed my dress, at the ankle, and did not see that I closed my eyes.

"Now, Raoul, you know the tragedy. It went on for two weeks. I burned his mask. He was my faithful slave. I gave him such confidence that he took me in the boat across the lake and let me through the gates that close the underground passages in the Rue Scribe. Here a carriage was waiting and took us to the woods. That night that we met you was very dangerous for me. He is very jealous of you. I had to tell him that you were soon going away. Then, after two weeks, he believed me when I said, 'I will come back!' "

"And you went back," Raoul said painfully. "You tell me that you love me, but you were free for only a few hours when you went back. Remember the masked party?"

"Yes, and those hours I spent with you were a great danger to both of us!"

"I doubted your love for me, during those hours."

"Do you doubt it still, Raoul? Each of my visits to Erik increase my horror of him! And I am so frightened!"

"But do you love me?" Raoul asked. "If Erik were good-looking, would you love me, Christine?"

She rose, put her arms around the young man's head, and said,

"If I did not love you, I would not give you my lips! Take them for the first time, and the last."

He kissed her and, as he did, the night broke like glass in a terrible storm. They ran away, their eyes wild with terror. High above them, the burning eyes of Erik stared down.

Chapter 7   A Mysterious Disappearance

Raoul and Christine did not stop until they came to the eighth floor. Suddenly, a strange-looking man blocked their way.

"No, not this way! Quick! Go away quickly!"

"Who is he? Who is that man?" Raoul asked, as Christine pulled him.

Christine answered, "It's the Persian."

"What's he doing here?"

"Nobody knows. He is always in the Opera."

When they were back in Christine's dressing room, she told Raoul that Erik had promised not to go behind the walls of her dressing room again. They spoke about their plans for the following night.

"After the performance, he will be waiting for you in the dining room on the lake, won't he?"

"Yes."

"How are you supposed to reach him?"

"I have the key to the gate to the underground passage in Rue Scribe. I can go straight to the edge of the lake."

"Give me the key, Christine."

"Never!" she said. Suddenly, she changed color. "Oh, Erik! Erik! Have pity on me!"

"What is it, Christine?"

"The ring ... the gold ring he gave me. When he gave it to me, he said, 'I will give you your freedom, but only on condition that this ring is always on your finger. If you ever take it off, you will suffer my revenge!' "

They both looked for the ring but could not find it.

"What will happen to us now? We can never find it!"

"Let's run away now," Raoul said firmly.

"No! Tomorrow!" she answered, and left him hurriedly.

♦

Raoul went home greatly upset, and as he went to bed that night he thought only about saving Christine. He thought of Erik, the monster.

Three times he shouted, "Curse him! . . . Curse him! . . . Curse him!"

But suddenly, he raised himself on his elbows. Two eyes, like burning coals, had appeared at the foot of his bed. They stared at him in the darkness of the night.

Raoul was not a coward, but he trembled. He put on his lamp and the eyes disappeared.

Raoul thought, "She told me that *his* eyes only showed in the dark. His eyes have disappeared in the light, but *he* may still be there."

He got up and looked under his bed, like a child. Then he thought he was being foolish and got into bed again and put out the lamp. The eyes reappeared.

He sat up and stared back at them and cried, "Is that you, Erik? Man, genius, or ghost, is it you?"

Raoul reached over and opened the drawer in the bedside table. He took out his gun and aimed at the two eyes. The shot made a terrible noise. Raoul could hear footsteps hurrying along the passages. The eyes disappeared. The servants and Count Philippe came running into his room, terribly anxious.

"What is it?" Philippe asked.

"I fired at two stars that stopped me from sleeping."

"Are you mad? Tell me, Raoul. What happened?"

"No, I'm not mad. Besides, we will soon see . . . " Raoul got up and looked out the window. "Look! Blood! See? That's a good thing! A ghost who bleeds is less dangerous!"

"Raoul! Raoul!" shouted the count, shaking him.

"You can see the blood. I wasn't dreaming. They weren't stars. They were Erik's eyes . . . and here is his blood!"

The servant brought a lamp and they examined outside the window. The blood went up the side of the house.

"My dear brother, you have fired at a cat," said Philippe.

Raoul continued to speak about the ghost and Erik, and both Philippe and the servant thought he was going mad. Later, when the judge received the report from the police, he thought the same thing.

"Who is Erik?" asked the count.

"He is my rival. And if he's not dead, it's a pity."

Raoul sent the servant away, but he heard Raoul say to the count, "I will carry off Christine Daaé tonight."

This phrase was afterward repeated to Monsieur Faure, the detective. But no one knew exactly what was said between the two brothers on that night. The servants said that this was not the first argument between the brothers. Their voices carried through the passages, and their arguments were always about an actress called Christine Daaé.

The next morning the count, who was having his breakfast in his study, sent for his brother. He handed Raoul a copy of the *Epoque* and said, "Read that!"

The newspaper reported a promise of marriage between Viscount Raoul Chagny and Mademoiselle Christine Daaé. It said that Count Philippe Chagny intended to prevent the marriage. The paper asked its readers if brotherly love would triumph over romantic love.

"You see, Raoul," said the count, "you are making us look

very foolish! Are you going with her tonight? Surely, you will not do anything so foolish? I *will* prevent you!"

"Goodbye, Philippe," said the viscount, and left the room.

The count did not see Raoul again until that evening, at the Opera, a few minutes before Christine's disappearance.

♦

Raoul spent all of that day preparing for the escape, and it kept him busy until nine o'clock at night. At that hour, a traveling carriage stopped outside the Opera next to the three carriages belonging to Carlotta, who was back in Paris, to Sorelli, and to Count Chagny. A shadow in a long black coat and a soft black hat passed by the carriages, examined the traveling carriage carefully, went up to the horse and driver, then moved away without saying a word.

The detective afterward believed that this shadow was Viscount Raoul Chagny. But I do not agree. The viscount always wore a tall hat, which was found later. I think the shadow was the ghost, who probably knew all about the escape, as the reader will soon find out.

The opera house was full and the viscount sat in a box, alone, listening to Christine in *Faust*. The audience, who had read the paragraph in that morning's *Epoque*, were not warm toward her, and she was losing her confidence more and more. Just then, Carlotta entered and poor Christine recognized her rival. The proud look on Carlotta's face gave Christine her confidence back. She forgot everything in order to triumph again.

She sang with all her heart and soul, and she succeeded in winning back her audience. A man stood up and remained standing, facing the singer. It was Raoul. She sang the words, "My spirit is desperate to rest with you!" And at that exact moment, the stage was suddenly in total darkness. Just as quickly, the lights came back on. But Christine Daaé was no longer there!

What had happened? Where had she gone? There was much confusion on the stage and in the audience. Raoul had cried out. Count Philippe had jumped up in his box. People looked at them and wondered if this event was connected in any way with the paragraph in the morning's paper. Raoul hurriedly left his seat, the count disappeared from his box, and everyone in the audience spoke at once, trying to suggest an explanation.

At last, the curtain rose and one of the singers said in a serious voice, "Christine Daaé has disappeared in front of our eyes... and nobody can tell us how!"

♦

Behind the curtain, there was a crowd of singers, dancers, scenery men—and all were asking questions and shouting. Three men stood together, talking in a low voice, looking desperately worried. They were Gabriel, the singing master, Mercier, the scenery manager, and Rémy, the secretary. They were anxious to tell the managers about Christine Daaé's disappearance. But the managers were in their office, and they had given orders that they were not to be bothered. Rémy made several attempts to persuade them to open the door of their office, and when he finally succeeded, Monsieur Moncharmin only shouted at him, "Do you have a safety pin?" When Rémy answered that he did not, Monsieur Moncharmin shouted at him to go away. Then he continued shouting for a safety pin until a boy brought him one, which he took—then quickly shut the door in Rémy's face.

Rémy returned to tell Gabriel and Mercier that he was unable to communicate the message of Christine Daaé's disappearance to the managers. Mercier decided to go and tell them himself.

Rémy questioned Gabriel about the managers' strange behavior earlier that evening. "Why won't they let anyone come near them or touch them?"

"What? Won't they? That is odd. What do you mean?"

"I saw them walking backward! And when I tried to shake Monsieur Richard's hand, Monsieur Moncharmin hurriedly whispered, 'Go away! Go away! Do not touch the manager!' Am I supposed to have a disease?"

"It's unbelievable!"

"Monsieur Richard turned around, and although there was no one in front of him, he put his hands together and lowered his head, and left slowly, walking backward!"

"Really?"

"And Monsieur Moncharmin also left, walking backward! They went like that to their office . . . backward! So, if they are not crazy, can you explain what this means?"

"Maybe they were practicing a dance for the ballet," suggested Gabriel, although he did not really believe this.

This made the secretary very angry. He whispered in Gabriel's ear, "There are things going on here and you and Mercier are partly responsible."

"What do you mean?" asked Gabriel.

"Christine Daaé is not the only one who disappeared tonight. Maybe you can explain why Mercier took Madame Giry away just a little while ago when she appeared in the hall?"

"Did he? I didn't see that."

"You did, Gabriel, because you went with Mercier and Madame Giry to Mercier's office. No one has seen Madame Giry since."

"Do you think we've eaten her?"

"No, but you locked her in the office."

Suddenly, Mercier arrived, out of breath. He told Gabriel and Rémy that he had knocked on the managers' office door and when Moncharmin appeared, he told him that Christine Daaé had disappeared. But Moncharmin said, "And a good thing, too!" Then, he put a safety pin into Mercier's hand.

"Strange! Very strange!" said Gabriel.

Suddenly, a voice made all three of them turn around. "I am sorry, gentlemen. Could you tell me where Christine Daaé is?"

The face was so white, so full of pain, that they were seized with pity. It was Viscount Chagny.

After Christine's disappearance, Raoul had rushed onto the stage and called her name. He ran to her dressing room, calling her name. Bitter tears burned his eyes as he looked at the clothes which she was supposed to wear that night for their escape. Why had she refused to leave earlier? Erik took her because he knew about their planned flight. Raoul thought of the eyes in his bedroom the night before. Why had he not killed him? He went to the mirror and pushed it, tried to find an opening, but the glass obeyed no one except Erik. He remembered something about a gate opening into the Rue Scribe from the lake, and he ran to the street. He could find no way to the lake, so he ran back inside, where he saw three men and asked them if they knew where Christine Daaé was.

At that moment another man appeared, and Mercier introduced Viscount Chagny to him.

"This is the man you should ask. Let me introduce Monsieur Mifroid, a police detective."

"I am delighted to meet you, Viscount Chagny. Would you mind coming with me? . . . And where are the managers? . . ."

Mercier did not answer, but Rémy told him that the managers were locked in their office.

"Let's go up to the office!" said Mifroid. He headed for the office with a growing crowd following behind him.

Mercier quickly put a key in Gabriel's hand and whispered, "This is all going very badly. You had better let Madame Giry out."

And Gabriel moved away.

"Open in the name of the law!" Mifroid shouted outside the managers' locked door. The door opened and everyone rushed in. Raoul was the last to enter. As he was following the others into the room, he heard these words spoken in his ear: "Erik's secrets concern no one except himself!"

He turned and saw a person with dark skin, green eyes, and wearing a wool cap. The Persian! The man held one finger over his lips. The viscount was surprised and speechless. The Persian disappeared.

Chapter 8   Twenty Thousand Francs and a Safety Pin

Earlier on the same day as the disappearance of Christine Daaé, the managers had received their second note from the ghost reminding them that his next monthly payment was due. It read:

> Do just as you did last month. It went very well. Put the 20,000 francs in the envelope and hand it to our excellent Madame Giry.

And with the note was the usual envelope. They only had to put the bills inside. This was done about a half an hour before the curtain rose on the first act of *Faust*. Then the managers called Madame Giry, who was back in her job as box-keeper, to their office. They wanted to ask her some questions.

Something mysterious had happened to that first envelope with 20,000 francs, and they did not want the same thing to happen again this month. But what had happened? Richard and Moncharmin had decided to tell Gabriel and Mercier about O.G.'s demand for an allowance. After putting the money into an envelope and watching Madame Giry take it to the ghost's box, the two managers and Gabriel and Mercier hid themselves and watched. They watched the envelope during the performance and afterward. But at last they became tired of waiting and watching, and they went to the ghost's box and opened it. The

20,000 francs were gone and had been replaced by twenty bills that were not real ones! Moncharmin had wanted to phone the police, but Richard had a plan. He told Moncharmin, "Let's not make ourselves look foolish. All of Paris would laugh at us. O.G. has won the first game; we will win the second."

He was thinking of the next month's allowance. And, we must not forget that these managers still suspected the last two managers of playing a joke on them. On the other hand, Moncharmin was sometimes troubled by doubts about Richard himself. They both had doubts about Madame Giry.

When Madame Giry arrived in their office on that day of Christine's disappearance, she did not have any idea that they suspected her of stealing last month's 20,000 francs.

"Madame Giry, do you know what is in this envelope?" Richard asked.

"Of course not," she said.

"Well, look."

"Thousand franc bills!" she cried.

"Yes, Madame Giry! And you knew it!"

"I, sir? I?"

"I am going to call the police and ask them to take you away!"

Madame Giry was shocked. "Call the police?"

"You are a thief, Madame Giry!"

She shouted angrily, "I have never heard of such a thing! And you, Monsieur Richard, know better than I where the 20,000 francs went to!"

"I? How should *I* know?"

Moncharmin, looking dissatisfied, demanded that the good lady explain herself.

Richard, who felt himself turning red under Moncharmin's eyes, shouted angrily at Madame Giry, "Why do you say that? Answer me!"

"Because the 20,000 francs went into *your* pocket!"

"In *his* pocket?" asked Moncharmin, whose hand stopped Richard's from hitting Madame Giry.

"You tell me that there were 20,000 francs in the envelope which I put into Monsieur Richard's pocket. But I tell you again, I knew nothing about it . . . nor Monsieur Richard either!"

"You see! I knew nothing either!"

Madame Giry continued to explain. She had slipped the envelope that Moncharmin had given her into Monsieur Richard's pocket on the evening that the Secretary for Fine Arts was visiting the Opera. The one that she took to the ghost's box was another envelope, just like it, which the ghost had given her and which she had hidden up her sleeve.

Madame Giry then reached into her sleeve and took out an envelope, like the one containing the 20,000 francs. They examined it and discovered that it, too, had twenty false bills. The ghost had told her to slip his envelope into Monsieur Richard's pocket. She then showed them how this was done. Moncharmin was amazed.

"It's a very good trick," said Richard. "So, he came and took the money from my pocket. I didn't notice—and I didn't know it was there! It's wonderful!"

"Oh, wonderful, no doubt!" Moncharmin agreed. "But you forget, Richard, that I provided 10,000 francs of the 20,000 and nobody put anything in *my* pocket!"

◆

On the evening that Rémy saw the managers acting very strangely, they had arranged that Richard would repeat the movements he had made on the evening that the 20,000 francs had disappeared.

Moncharmin was watching Richard's pocket, where Madame Giry was going to put 20,000 francs. Richard stood in the same spot where he had stood when he showed his admiration and respect for the Secretary for Fine Arts. Moncharmin stood behind him. Madame Giry rubbed against Monsieur Richard, slipped the envelope into his coat pocket, and disappeared. Mercier, following Moncharmin's instructions, took the good lady to the scenery manager's office and turned the key, making it impossible for her to communicate with her ghost.

Richard, during this time, was walking backward, imagining he had the Secretary of Fine Arts in front of him, which caused amazement to those who saw him.

Moncharmin did the same thing, in addition to pushing away Rémy and begging the manager of the Central Bank not to touch him. Moncharmin did not want Richard to come to him when the 20,000 francs were gone and say, "Maybe it was the manager of the Central Bank . . . or Rémy."

The two managers returned to their office in this way, walking backward, with Moncharmin keeping a close watch behind Richard. They locked themselves in the office and Moncharmin put the key in his pocket.

"We remained locked up like this last time," he said, "until you left the Opera to go home."

"No one came in, I suppose?"

"No one."

"Then I was robbed on the way home from the Opera."

"No, that's impossible. I gave you a ride home. The 20,000 francs disappeared at your place: there's no doubt about that."

"Not *my* servants!"

Moncharmin raised his eyes—he did not wish to discuss details.

"Moncharmin, I've had enough of this!" said Richard, tired of his partner's attitude.

"Richard, *I've* had enough of this!"

"Do you dare to suspect me?"

"Yes, of a silly joke!"

"One does not joke with 20,000 francs."

"That's what I think!"

"Look, you gave me a ride. You were the only one to approach me. If the 20,000 francs was no longer in my pocket, there's a good chance of it being in yours!"

Moncharmin jumped up at the suggestion. "Oh!" he shouted. "A safety pin!"

"What do you want a safety pin for?"

"To fasten the 20,000 francs to your coat! Then you will feel the hand that pulls at your pocket and you will see if it's mine! Oh, so you are suspecting me now, are you? A safety pin!"

And that was the moment when Moncharmin opened the door and shouted down the passage, "A safety pin! Somebody give me a safety pin!"

This, of course, was when Rémy saw Moncharmin and the boy who brought the safety pin, which Moncharmin took before shutting the door in Rémy's face. Then, Moncharmin knelt down behind Richard. He took the envelope from Richard's pocket and took out the bills with a trembling hand. He made sure they were real, then pinned them back in the coat pocket with great care. Then he sat down behind Richard's coattails and kept his eyes on them, while Richard, sitting at his writing table, did not move.

"The clock will soon strike twelve," said Moncharmin. "Last time, we left at twelve."

"And if it is a ghost who puts the magic envelopes on the table," said Richard, "... who talks in Box Five ... who killed Joseph Buquet ... who unhooked the chandelier ... and who robs us ... There is no one here except you and me. If the bills disappear and neither you nor I are involved, we will have to believe in the ghost."

At that moment the clock began to strike twelve times. The two managers trembled, their foreheads were wet. When the clock stopped, they rose from their chairs.

"Before we go, do you mind if I look in your pocket?" asked Moncharmin.

"You must!"

As Moncharmin was feeling the pocket, Richard asked, "Well?"

"I can feel the pin."

"Of course, as you said, we can't be robbed without noticing it."

But Moncharmin shouted, "I can feel the pin, but I *can't* feel the bills!"

Richard pulled off his coat. The two managers turned the pocket inside out. *The pocket was empty.* But the pin remained in the same place. There was no longer any doubt.

"The ghost," whispered Moncharmin.

But Richard jumped on his partner. "No one except you has touched my pocket! Give me back my 20,000 francs!"

"I swear I don't have it."

Then somebody knocked at the door. Moncharmin opened it automatically. He hardly recognized Mercier, exchanged a few words with him without knowing what he was saying and, with an unconscious movement, put the safety pin into the hands of his puzzled scenery manager.

Chapter 9   Raoul Follows the Persian

Police detective Mifroid entered the managers' office and asked, "Is Christine Daaé here?"

"Why do you ask if Christine Daaé is here?" asked Richard.

"Because she has to be found."

"Has she disappeared?"

"In the middle of the performance."

"This is extraordinary!"

"Isn't it? And what is *quite* extraordinary is that you are learning it from me!"

"Yes," said Richard, taking his head in his hands and saying to himself, "It's enough to make a man give up." He looked up and said to the detective, "So she . . . she disappeared in the middle of the performance?"

"Yes, carried off at the moment she was asking the angels to take her away. But I doubt she was carried off by an angel."

"And *I* am sure she was!"

Everybody looked at the young man, pale and trembling with excitement, who repeated, "I am sure of it!"

"Sure of what?" asked Mifroid.

"Christine Daaé was carried off by an angel, and I can tell you his name!"

The detective asked everyone to leave except the managers and the viscount. Then Raoul spoke. "Sir, the angel is called Erik. He lives in the Opera and he is the Angel of Music!"

Mifroid turned to the managers and asked, "Do you have an Angel of Music in the opera house, gentlemen?"

Richard and Moncharmin shook their heads, without even speaking.

"These gentlemen know him as the Opera ghost, who is the same person as the Angel of Music, and his real name is Erik," explained Raoul.

"Gentlemen, do you know the Opera ghost?"

Richard stood and said, "No, sir, we do not know him, but we would like to. Because this evening he robbed us of 20,000 francs!"

And Richard turned a terrible look on Moncharmin and said, "Give me back the 20,000 francs, or I'll tell the whole story."

Moncharmin said, "Oh, tell him everything."

Mifroid looked at Raoul and at the two managers and wondered if he were in a madhouse.

"OK," said Mifroid. "The singer first, then the 20,000 francs. Monsieur Chagny, you believe that Christine Daaé was carried off by an individual called Erik. Do you know this person? Have you seen him?"

"Yes."

"Where?"

"In a churchyard."

Raoul told them about Perros-Guirec, the face of Death, the violin. They all thought he was completely mad. Just as Raoul finished, the door opened and a man entered. It was a detective with an important message for Mifroid, who listened to the detective without taking his eyes off Raoul.

"Monsieur," said Mifroid to Raoul, "let's talk about you now. Were you planning to carry off Mademoiselle Christine Daaé tonight?"

"Yes, sir."

"After the performance?"

"Yes, sir."

"All your arrangements were made?"

"Yes, sir."

Mifroid continued his questioning. He asked Raoul if his brother were opposed to these arrangements, and if Raoul knew that his brother's carriage was no longer in front of the opera house. "Monsieur Chagny, I must inform you that your brother has been smarter than you!" the detective said. "He is the one who carried off Christine Daaé!"

"Oh, impossible! Are you sure?" the poor young man asked.

"He has taken her in his carriage across Paris and out of Paris . . . by the Brussels road."

"I shall catch them!" cried Raoul, and he rushed out of the office.

"And bring her back to us!" cried the detective happily. "That's a trick worth two of the Angel of Music's!" And, turning to the other men, Monsieur Mifroid told them that no one was more anxious to find Christine than the younger Monsieur Chagny. He smiled. "This is, gentlemen, the art of the police. It consists of getting police work done by other people!"

But Monsieur Mifroid would not have been quite so satisfied with himself if he had known that his assistant was stopped at the entrance to the first passage. A tall figure blocked Raoul's way. "Where are you going so fast, Monsieur Chagny?"

"It's you!" he cried in a feverish voice. "You, who know Erik's secrets and don't want me to speak of them! Who are you?"

"You know who I am! I am the Persian!"

The man with the dark skin and green eyes, wearing a wool cap, bent over Raoul. Raoul remembered that his brother had once pointed to this mysterious person and told him that he was a Persian who lived in an apartment in the Rue de Rivoli. Again, the Persian asked Raoul where he was going.

"To Christine Daaé's assistance!"

"Then, sir, stay here. Christine Daaé is here!"

"With Erik?"

"With Erik."

"How do you know?"

"I was at the performance and no one in the world except Erik could steal someone like that!"

"Can you help me find her?"

"I can try to take you to her . . . and to him."

"How can I not believe you, when you are the only one to believe me . . . when you are the only one not to smile when Erik's name is mentioned?" said Raoul.

"We must not mention that name here. Let's say 'he' and 'him;' there will be less danger of attracting his attention."

"Do you think he is near us?"

"It is quite possible, sir, if he is not at this moment with his prisoner, *in the house on the lake.*"

"So you know that house, too?"

"If he is not there, he may be here, in this wall, in this floor, in this ceiling! Come!"

Raoul followed the Persian up and down stairs that he had never seen before. They came to a door which the Persian opened with a key. There, they were met by a stranger with dark skin and a cap like the Persian's. He gave a box to the Persian. "Thank you, Darius. Did anyone see you?"

"No, master."

"Let no one see you go out."

The Persian's servant quickly disappeared down the passageway. The Persian opened the box and inside there were two guns. "When Christine disappeared, I asked my servant to bring me these guns. Here, take this one. Hold it up, ready to shoot at all times. Hold it up in front of your face. We must be prepared for anything because we shall be fighting the most terrible rival that you can imagine."

"You must hate Erik!"

"No, sir," said the Persian sadly, "I do not hate him. If I had ever hated him, he would have long ago stopped doing harm."

"Has he done you harm?"

"I have forgiven him for the harm he has done to me." The Persian spoke with great pity in his voice, just as Christine had. He took Raoul to Christine's dressing room and went straight to the mirror.

"Are we going out by the mirror?" Raoul asked.

"So you knew that Christine went out by that mirror?"

"I watched her. I was hidden behind the curtain of the inner room and I watched her disappear."

The Persian pressed his hands against the glass. He was trying to move it. Raoul watched. The Persian explained the complicated system, but he was having trouble making it work. "Maybe he cut the cord so that we couldn't turn it," said the Persian.

"Why would he? He doesn't know that we are coming."

"He suspects it, I'm sure. He knows that I understand the system."

"It's not turning!...And Christine, sir, Christine?" Raoul asked nervously in a trembling voice.

"We will do all that is humanly possible. But he commands the walls, the doors, and the trap doors. In my country, he was known as 'the trap door lover!'"

"But why do these walls obey only him? He did not build them!"

"Yes, sir, that is just what he did!" The Persian pulled Raoul close to him and said, "And now, look out! And be ready to shoot!"

They raised their guns opposite the glass; it turned on its center like the door to a restaurant or store. As it turned, it carried Raoul and the Persian with it and suddenly threw them from the full, blinding light into the deepest darkness.

"Follow me and do all that I do," said the Persian, who took a small light from his pocket and turned it on.

They were in a passage made of wood and went on their knees until they came to an opening. The Persian dropped down first, then Raoul. The faint light was just enough to let Raoul see the shape of things around him. And he could not hold back a small cry when he saw three dead bodies.

Suddenly, there were voices. One voice was police detective Mifroid's and he was talking to the stage manager. They, too, saw the bodies. Raoul and the Persian kept back in the dark and listened to the discussion. The bodies were those of Mauclair, the chief gas man in charge of lighting (as electricity was not yet used much), and his two assistants. The stage manager thought they were dead, but Mifroid quickly realized that they were not, but were drugged and in a deep sleep. He told the stage manager to call a doctor, then he asked the managers, "What do you say to all this, gentlemen?" The managers stood with surprised faces at the top of the stairs, and in fact had very little to say.

The stage manager, who was still standing there, said, "This is not the first time that Mauclair has fallen asleep in the theater. I remember finding him once before."

"When was that?"

"The night when Carlotta—you know, sir—gave her famous '*Co-ack*'!"

"Really?" asked Mifroid, staring hard at the stage manager.

Raoul and the Persian watched as the bodies were taken away, then the Persian took Raoul down to the third cellar. It was a long way up and down stairs and through narrow passages, and they heard many strange and frightening noises along the way. When they came to the spot where Joseph Buquet had been found hanging, the Persian pressed against the wall and a stone fell, leaving a hole through which the two men passed.

"Take off your shoes. We shall get them when we leave," the Persian said. He went a little farther on his knees, then said, "I am going to hang by my hands from the edge of the stone and let myself drop *into his house*. You must do exactly the same. Do not be afraid. I will catch you in my arms."

They dropped down as the Persian said, and stood still, listening. The darkness was thick around them; the silence was heavy and terrible. The Persian held up his light and looked for the hole through which they had dropped, but it had closed up. Then he noticed something like a cord on the ground, and he bent down to pick it up. He examined it for a moment, then, in horror, threw it away. It was a Punjab rope—maybe the one that had been used around Buquet's neck. The Persian knew how skillful Erik was with this rope. He had seen it before.

Anxiously, he looked around, then with deep emotion he whispered, "We have dropped into the torture room!"

Chapter 10   The Persian's Story

When I began searching for the truth about this extraordinary tragedy involving Count Chagny, his brother the viscount, and Christine Daaé, I had the good fortune to meet Detective Faure. He told me all about the Persian, who still lived in Rue de Rivoli, and I went to visit him. He gave me some documents, including this report of events that happened in the torture room. The words here are exactly as he wrote them:

It was the first time that I had entered the house on the lake. I had often begged "the trap door lover" to open its mysterious doors to me. He always refused. After he started living in the Opera, I tried to watch and learn as he worked the door in the wall on the lake, but it was too dark to see. One day, when I thought I was alone, I took the boat out on the lake toward the part of the wall where I had seen Erik disappear.

In the lake I heard singing, beautiful singing, beside me in the water. The lake was perfectly calm and I knew that it had to be a new invention of Erik's. But this invention was so perfect that I leaned out of the boat, charmed by the voice, and suddenly two arms came out of the water and seized me around the neck, dragging me down with great force. I cried out. Erik knew it was me, and instead of drowning me as he had planned, he swam with me and laid me on the shore.

He told me I was foolish and that he did not want me, or anybody, there. And he asked me, "Did you save my life only to make it unbearable for me?"

I didn't answer. I wanted to know how he had managed the trick of the singing lake, and he agreed to satisfy my curiosity. There is nothing he loves more, after surprising people, than to prove how mysteriously his mind works. I knew this because I had known him in Persia. I also knew that he was a monster.

He showed me a useful trick for breathing, and singing, under water. "It's a trick that nearly killed me!" I said. "And you know what you promised me, Erik? No more murders!"

"Have I really committed murders?" he asked in a friendly voice.

"Have you forgotten? But that is the past . . . and you are responsible to me for the present because, if I had wished, you would have died long ago. Remember that, Erik. I saved your life!"

When I asked him about the chandelier, he laughed a most terrible laugh and said, "The chandelier was old and needed repairs, my dear *daroga*!★ It just fell. Now go and dry yourself. And never get into my boat again. And do not try to get into my house!" Then he disappeared in the darkness of the lake.

Ever since I discovered that Erik was living in the Opera, I feared for everyone. When people said, "It's the ghost!", I thought, "I would not be surprised if it were Erik." I knew what this devil could do. His terrible ugliness put him outside the rest of humanity. It seemed to me that for that reason he no longer believed that he had any duty toward the human race.

When he told me that he was loved for himself, I hid in the room next to Christine Daaé's dressing room and listened to his singing. I could not understand how she could love such a terribly ugly person until I learned that she had not yet seen him! At this time I also discovered the trick that made the wall with the mirror swing around, and how the walls were built of hollow bricks so that his voice easily carried into her room. And I discovered the trap door that allowed him to go straight to the cellars below.

One day, when he caught me spying on him, he said, "If my secrets stop being my secrets, it will be a bad day for many people!"

★ *daroga*: the Persian word for chief of police.

When I accused him of carrying off Christine Daaé and keeping her locked up in his house, he told me that he could prove to me that she loved him. He said he would let her go, and I would see her return to him because she loved him and wanted to return. He told me that it would end in a marriage.

I said that if I saw her do this, I would no longer bother him or follow him around. So he told me to watch that night when they went to the masked party. And, to my surprise, things happened as he said they would. She left the house on the lake and returned to it several times.

I was very interested in this relationship with Christine Daaé. I was worried by the terrible thought of what Erik would do if he found that he was not loved for himself, as he imagined. Soon I learned the truth about the monster's love affair.

He filled Christine's mind, but the girl's heart belonged to Viscount Chagny. While they played around on the upper floors of the Opera to avoid the monster, they did not suspect that I was watching them. I was prepared to do anything—to kill the monster, if necessary.

I thought that the monster would be driven away from his house by jealousy, and this would allow me to enter it. It was important that I knew what was inside. One day, tired of waiting for an opportunity, I discovered the stone in the wall that could be taken out and put back. I moved the stone and heard that devil, Erik, working on his piece of music—his *Don Juan Triumphant*. I knew that this was the work of his life.

On the day that Christine Daaé disappeared during her performance, I had read about her possible marriage to Viscount Chagny and I feared what might happen. So I was certain that she had been taken away by Erik, prince of magicians. I wanted to tell everyone to leave the Opera because I was afraid of what might happen next. But I stopped myself. That was when I decided that I must go to his house, where he had certainly taken her. I decided to take that poor little desperate viscount, and I sent my servant for my guns. The viscount trusted me completely, but my fear was great that Erik was near and preparing the Punjab rope.

No one knows better than Erik how to throw the Punjab rope. He used to amuse the Persian princess in her palace, Mazenderan, with his rope-throwing tricks. He had lived in India, where he learned to throw a rope like a cowboy and could use it to kill men. This is why I told the viscount to hold his gun up in front of his face. I knew that it would be very difficult for Erik to throw his rope around our necks if our arms were held up in front of them.

When the viscount and I arrived at last in the third cellar, I moved the stone and we jumped into the house which Erik had built himself in the walls of the Opera. Erik had worked under Philippe Garnier, the architect of the Opera, after returning to France. He continued to work by himself when the building of the Opera was stopped during the war.

I knew what this house was probably like because I had seen what he had done in Mazenderan. With his trap doors, the monster was responsible for endless tragedies of all kinds. He made unbelievable inventions, but the most curious and terrible was the torture room. If the princess wanted someone killed, she sent them to Erik's torture room.

The room Monsieur Chagny and I dropped into was exactly the same as Erik's previous torture room. At our feet was the Punjab rope which I had been worrying about all evening. I suspected that it was this rope that killed Joseph Buquet, probably when he found Erik moving the stone in the third cellar. Erik probably dragged Buquet's body to where it was found, and threw the rope down into the torture room to hide it.

I am not a coward, but when I found it . . . I felt sick. Monsieur Chagny noticed and asked me what was wrong. I put my finger to my lips to warn him to be silent.

The room was full of mirrors and we could hear Erik's voice as he spoke to Christine Daaé. I was certain that Erik did not know of our presence because if he had, the tortures would have begun at once. I feared that Viscount Chagny, who wanted to rush through the walls to Christine, might not be able to control himself.

We heard Erik say to her, "*Don Juan Triumphant* is finished, and now I want to live like everybody else. I want to have a wife like everybody else. I have invented a mask that makes me look like anybody else. People will not even turn around in the streets. You will be the happiest of women. You are crying! You are afraid of me! But I am not really cruel. Love me and you will see! If you loved me, I would be very gentle, and you could do anything with me that you pleased."

We heard desperate cries, which we soon realized were from Erik. Christine seemed to be standing dumb with horror, without the strength to cry out, while the monster was on his knees in front of her.

"You don't love me!" he cried three times.

Then, strangely, there was the sound of an electric bell. Erik got up and walked across the room. We heard a door close. Christine was now alone, behind the wall! The viscount called to her, "Christine! Christine!"

Her faint voice reached us. "I am dreaming!" she said.

Raoul told her that we were there to save her. She said that Erik had gone mad with love. He would kill everybody including himself if she did not agree to become his wife. He had told her that if her answer was no, everybody would be dead and buried. He had given her until eleven o'clock the next evening to think about it. She had to choose the music—wedding music or funeral music.

I asked her if she knew where Erik had gone. She thought he had left the house.

"Can you open the door?" I asked her, because we could not see a door between the torture room and the sitting room she was in. But she was tied to her chair and could not move. Erik had tied her up after she had tried to kill herself; she had banged her head against the floor several times. I asked her where the key was and she told me it was in a leather bag that Erik called the bag of life and death. Suddenly, she told us that he was coming.

"Ask him to untie you. Tell him it hurts. Remember, he loves you, Christine."

And when Erik entered, she begged him to untie her, which he did. He sat down and began to play some slow, sad music and his voice poured out the funeral song. Suddenly, he stopped and the voice, totally changed, demanded angrily, "What have you done with my bag? You wanted me to untie you so that you could take my bag!" She had managed to take it while he was playing. As he took the bag back from her, Christine made a cry of pain. Hearing this, Raoul could not hold back his anger, or his own bitter cry.

"What's that? Did you hear something, Christine?" said the terrible creature.

"No, I heard nothing," replied the poor girl.

"I thought I heard a cry."

"A cry! Are you going mad, Erik? I cried out because you hurt me! I heard nothing."

"I don't like the way you said that! You're trembling. You're lying! There was a cry! There is someone in the torture room! I understand now!"

"There is no one there, Erik!"

"The man you want to marry, maybe!"

"I don't want to marry anybody! You know I don't!"

"It won't take long to find out. If there is someone in there, you will see a window light up near the ceiling. If we pull back the black curtain and put out the light in here . . ."

And that was when it began—the thing I feared most. We were suddenly flooded with light.

The angry voice shouted, "I told you there was someone! Do you see the window now? The lighted window, right up there?" The devil told Christine to go up the steps and look through the window, down into the torture room. I do not know if the viscount heard her trembling voice because his full attention was taken by the unbelievable world he found himself in. I had seen this sight too often, through the little window in the palace in Mazenderan.

I heard Christine ask, "Why do you call that room the torture room?"

"What did you see through the window?"

"I saw a forest," she answered. "But there was no one there— only trees."

"You see? It's all a joke! But I am very tired of it! I am tired of having a forest and a torture room in my house. I want to live like other people. I want a nice, quiet apartment with ordinary doors and windows and a wife inside it! My dear little Christine! Are you listening to me? Tell me you love me! No, you don't love me, but you will! You will get used to me. You would have lots of fun with me. I am the greatest ventriloquist that ever lived. I am the first ventriloquist in the world! You're laughing ... Maybe you don't believe me? Listen."

The devil, who really was the first ventriloquist in the world, was only trying to take the girl's attention away from the torture room. But it was a stupid plan because she thought of nothing except us.

"Put out the light in the little window, Erik," she said.

She knew that this light must mean something terrible. One thing that calmed her fears a little was the sight of us in that light, alive and well. But she wanted the light put out.

Chapter 11　The Scorpion or the Grasshopper

"Listen, dear. My mouth is closed, but you can hear my voice," said the ventriloquist. "See the two boxes on the shelf? My voice is in the little box on the right. What is it saying? *Shall I turn the scorpion?* And now, what is it saying in the little box on the left? *Shall I turn the grasshopper?* Here it is in the little bag. What is it saying? *I am the little bag of life and death!* And now it's in Carlotta's throat! *Co-ack!* It's on a chair in the ghost's box and it is saying, *Madame Carlotta is singing tonight to bring the chandelier down!* Where is Erik's voice now? Listen, Christine, my dear. It's behind the door of the torture room. It's me in the torture room! And what am I saying? *Look out if you have a nose, a real nose, and have come to look around the torture room!*"

Oh, the ventriloquist's terrible voice! It was everywhere, everywhere! It ran around us, between us! Erik was there, speaking to us! We jumped across the room to catch him, but his voice jumped back, behind the wall! Soon we heard nothing more because this is what happened:

"Erik! Erik!" said Christine's voice. "Stop! I'm tired of this. Isn't it very hot here?"

"Oh, yes," replied Erik's voice. "The heat is unbearable."

"But what does this mean? The wall is really getting hot! The wall is burning!"

"I'll tell you, Christine. It is the forest next door. Didn't you see it was an African forest?"

And the devil laughed so loudly and terribly that we could no longer hear Christine's cries. Viscount Chagny shouted and banged against the walls like a madman. I could not stop him. And then there was the sound of a body falling on the floor and being dragged along. A door banged and then nothing. Nothing more around us except the burning silence of a tropical forest.

Our prison had six walls completely covered in mirrors.

These rooms are not unusual today, but the invention belongs to Erik, who built the first room of this kind under my eyes at that time in Mazenderan in Persia. But the Persian princess grew tired of this, so Erik changed his invention into a torture room. He put an iron tree with painted leaves in one corner. The attacks of the person in the torture room could not destroy it. There was only this tree and nothing else, except the electric heating system, which could be controlled. The mirrors multiplied the tree so that it gave the impression of a tropical forest under a burning sun.

The viscount was in a terrible state of worry. He rubbed his forehead with his hands, hoping to drive away a bad dream. He opened and shut his eyes, but the forest did not disappear.

I noticed that the mirrors were marked and scratched, which proved to me that this torture room had already served a purpose. Yes, someone driven crazy in this room had kicked those mirrors. And the branch of the tree where he had put an end to his own suffering was arranged so that, before dying, he had seen a thousand men suffering with him. Yes, Joseph Buquet had undoubtedly experienced all this! Were we to die as he had done? I did not think so. I knew we had a few hours, and I could use my knowledge of Erik's "tricks" to try to find a way out.

We had dropped too far down to go back the way we came. The only possible way out was through the door that led to the room where Erik had kept Christine. Although this door could be seen by Christine, it was impossible to see from inside the torture room. We had to try to open it without even knowing where it was.

I had to calm the viscount, who was already walking about like a man going mad. His worry for Christine, the magic forest, and the burning heat were having their intended effect on his brain. I made him touch the mirrors and the iron tree, and I explained to him what was happening. I promised to find the door, but he had to let me search. I told him that he must not shout and walk up and down, so he lay on the floor, as one does in a forest.

I placed my fingers on the mirrors, hunting for the weak point. I tried not to lose a minute, as I was feeling more and more faint from the heat.

After half an hour, the viscount interrupted my search. "Do you think you will find it soon? If it takes much longer, we will be roasted alive!"

I was sorry to hear him talk like this. I had hoped that his sense of reason would last some time longer against the torture. Then, he told me that it was a comfort to know that if we could not get out and save Christine, at least we would be dead before her!

I continued my search, but I was having no luck. We were both very thirsty. Fear was growing in our hearts—of the wild animals in the forest. Erik's tricks included the sounds of lions and other dangerous animals, but this knowledge was little comfort. After a while, I was so tired that I threw myself down beside the viscount. I knew that, by now, Erik knew who was in the torture room. I called him: "Erik! Erik!"

There was no answer. We were beginning to die of heat, hunger, and thirst. The viscount sat up and pointed to a spot. "Water!" he shouted. I knew this trick, and did not want to hope. If a man hoped for water, he would pull himself desperately. . . to the mirror. Then there was only one thing for him to do—to hang himself on the iron tree.

I tried to stop the viscount, but he no longer believed what I said. He dragged himself forward, saying, "Water! Water!"

His mouth was open and he thought he was drinking. And my mouth was open, too. We not only saw the water, we heard it.

Finally—and this was the most pitiless torture of all—we heard the rain and it was not raining. Another trick of Erik's, which he managed by dropping small stones into a box he had made for this purpose. When we reached the mirror, with our tongues out, Viscount Chagny put his tongue against the glass, and I put my tongue against the glass.

It was burning hot!

We rolled on the floor in terrible hopelessness. Viscount Chagny put his gun to his head, and I stared at the Punjab rope at the foot of the iron tree. Suddenly, I saw something and I jumped, which delayed the viscount's attempt to shoot himself. I took his arm. And then I took the gun from him . . . and dragged myself to what I had seen.

Near the Punjab rope there was a black nail, and I recognized its use. I pushed the nail and a trap door opened. Cool air came up to us from the black hole below. I put my arm in and felt . . . stairs . . . stairs leading to a cellar.

We went down and found ourselves in Erik's cellar, where we hoped to find wine. Erik likes fine wines. But instead we found something terrible! Now I understood what that devil meant when he said to Christine, "Yes or no! If your answer is no, everybody will be dead *and buried*!"

He had chosen his time well—eleven o'clock at night. We were all going to die—Christine, the viscount, me, the performers, and the audience—in a terrible explosion in the middle of a performance in the Paris Opera if Christine Daaé said no! The cellar was full of powder that would explode if she refused to marry Erik!

Christine did not know that the lives of so many people depended on her acceptance or refusal. And how could she not refuse? But what time was it? We had no idea how much time we had spent in the torture room, and it was too dark to see our watches. We climbed back up the stairs and into the torture room, which was now as dark as the cellar. We called out: Viscount Chagny called to Christine and I to Erik. But there was no answer. Viscount Chagny broke the glass of his watch and felt the two hands. Judging by the space between the hands, he thought it might be just eleven o'clock! But which eleven o'clock—morning or night? And which day?

Suddenly, I heard footsteps in the next room. Someone knocked lightly on the wall. Christine's voice said, "Raoul! Raoul!"

We were now all talking at once, on the two sides of the wall. Afraid that he might be dead, Christine cried when she heard Raoul's voice.

"What is the time now?" Raoul asked her. "Quickly, Christine!"

"It's five minutes to eleven," she replied. "He has given me five minutes to decide. Before he went out he said, 'Here is the key that opens the little boxes in the sitting room. In one of the boxes, you will find a scorpion, in the other, a grasshopper. If you turn the scorpion around, that will mean your answer is yes. The grasshopper will mean no.' And he laughed like a drunk devil. I begged him to give me the key to the torture room. I said I would marry him if he gave it to me. He laughed again and left me. His last words were, 'The grasshopper! A grasshopper does not only turn, it jumps! It jumps! And it jumps very high!' "

I understood. If the grasshopper were turned, it would jump—it controlled an electricity supply that would cause the explosion.

Viscount Chagny quickly explained the situation to Christine in a few hurried words, and he told her to turn the scorpion immediately. But, as she went to follow his instruction, I shouted, "Don't touch it!" The idea had come to me—I knew my Erik—that maybe he had deceived the girl once more. Maybe it was the scorpion that would blow everything up. Why wasn't he there? The five minutes had passed and he was not back. Had he found shelter for himself as he waited for the explosion? Why had he not returned?

"Here he comes!" cried Christine. "I can hear him!"

We heard him enter the sitting room. He walked toward Christine, but did not speak.

"Erik! It is I! Do you know me?" I shouted.

With extraordinary calmness, he answered, "So you are not dead in there? Well, keep quiet."

I tried to speak, but he said coldly, "Not a word, *daroga*, or I will blow everything up." Then he said to Christine, "If you turn the grasshopper, mademoiselle, we will all be blown up. There is enough powder in the cellar to blow up a whole district of Paris. If you turn the scorpion, the powder will be drowned in water. To celebrate our wedding, you will give a lot of people a great present—their lives. With your own hands, you will. turn the scorpion . . . and happily, happily, we will be married! You have two minutes, then I will turn the grasshopper. And I tell you, the grasshopper *jumps very high!*"

"Erik, do you swear to me that the scorpion is the one to turn?" she cried.

"Yes, the scorpion . . ." he said, moving his fingers slowly toward the grasshopper in a successful attempt to frighten her.

"Erik! I have turned the scorpion!"

Oh, the second we passed through, waiting to find ourselves in little pieces in the middle of the terrible ruins. Suddenly, we heard a noise below us. It was the sound of water. All of our thirst, which had disappeared when the terror came, now returned with the sound of the water. The viscount and I went down to the cellar and drank. The water rose and we went back up to the torture room, where the water was entering and forming a little lake. It continued to rise. We called out to Erik and Christine, but there was no answer. The water was moving around and around and we were going with it. Were we going to drown here in the torture room?

"Erik! Erik!" I shouted. "I saved your life! Remember! You were going to die! If it weren't for me, you would be dead now! Erik!"

There was no reply. Then I lost consciousness.

Chapter 12   Erik—Phantom, Monster, or Man?

That was the end of the Persian's story as he wrote it.

Viscount Chagny and the Persian were saved by Christine Daaé. I heard the rest of the story from the lips of the *daroga* himself. When I went to see him, he was a very sick, old man and it was very difficult to persuade him to relive the tragedy for me.

It seems that when he opened his eyes, the *daroga* found himself lying on a bed. Christine brought him a drink, but she did not say a word. Erik was looking at him.

"Are you better, *daroga*?" Erik asked him. He pointed to the viscount and said, "He woke up long before we knew if you were still alive. He is quite well. He is asleep. We must not wake him. You are saved, both of you. And soon I will take you up to the surface of the earth, *to please my wife*." Then, he left the room.

Christine sat in a corner, reading a book. The Persian tried to speak to her, but she did not look up. Eventually, the Persian fell asleep and did not wake again until he was in his own room, with his faithful Darius at his bedside. Darius told him that a stranger had left him on his doorstep the night before.

As soon as he was well enough, the Persian sent a message to Count Philippe's house asking about the viscount's health. The answer was that the young man had not been seen and that Count Philippe was dead. The count's body was found next to the Opera lake, on the Rue Scribe side. The Persian had no doubt concerning the crime or the criminal. He was sure that the count had gone looking for his brother, had found the lake, and had been pulled in. The Persian informed the police. The detective, Monsieur Faure, thought he was mad.

Desperate, the Persian sat down and wrote the story that you have just read. He thought that the newspapers might be interested in it. When he had just written the last line, Darius announced that a visitor, who refused to give his name or show his face, wanted to see the *daroga*. The Persian knew who this must be and told Darius to let him in.

The Persian rose as Erik entered. Erik looked weak and leaned against the wall.

"Murderer of Count Philippe, what have you done with his brother and Christine Daaé?"

Erik, who could hardly speak, told the Persian that Count Philippe's death was an accident—that he had fallen into the lake. And that now, he, too, was dying.

"Of love, *daroga*...I am dying of love. And I still love her. If you knew how beautiful she was when she let me kiss her... alive...It was the first time I ever kissed a woman...I kissed her alive and she looked so beautiful!"

"Is she alive now?" the Persian asked angrily.

"Yes, yes, she is alive. She saved your life, *daroga*. How she begged me to save her little friend! She promised to be my wife if I would save him, and she looked so beautiful. That was when I knew she would be my living wife. Until then, I had always seen my dead wife in her eyes. It was the first time I saw my living wife there. She would not kill herself. Half a minute later, the water was back in the lake. I carried you out of the house and left you at your door."

"What did you do with Viscount Chagny?" the Persian asked.

"I wanted to keep him, but not in the house. So, I tied him up and left him in the emptiest part of the Opera, below the fifth cellar, where no one ever comes, and where no one ever hears you. Then I went back to Christine. She was waiting for me."

Erik rose, but he trembled like a leaf. He continued, "Yes, she was waiting for me. And when I came forward, she did not run away... and I kissed her on the forehead! Oh, how good it is to kiss somebody on the forehead! My mother, *daroga*, my poor, unhappy mother never... let me kiss her... She used to run away... and throw me my mask! There has never been any other woman ... ever, ever! My happiness was so great, I cried. I fell at her feet, crying... and I kissed her feet... her little feet... crying... You're crying, too, *daroga*!"

The Persian could not hold back his tears as he looked at that masked man, who was holding his heart and crying with pain and love at the same time.

"Her tears fell on my forehead and they mixed with my tears... Listen, *daroga*, listen to what I did!... I tore off my mask and she did not run away!... And she did not die!... We cried together! I have tasted all the happiness the world can offer! While I was at her feet I heard her say, 'Poor, unhappy Erik!'... *And she took my hand!*... I held in my hand a ring, a plain gold ring which I had given her... and she had lost... and which I found again... I slipped it into her little hand and said, 'There! Take it! Take it for you... and him! It will be my wedding present from your poor, unhappy Erik! I know you love the boy!' ... She asked me what I meant... I told her she could marry the young man... because she had cried with me and mixed her tears with mine! I freed the young man... He and Christine kissed in front of me... I made Christine swear to come back, one night, when I was dead, crossing the lake from the Rue Scribe side, and to bury me with the gold ring, which she would wear until that moment... I told her where she would find my body and what to do with it... Then Christine kissed me, for the first time, herself, here, on the forehead, and they went off together... *Daroga*, if Christine keeps her promise, she will come back soon!"

Before he left, Erik told the *daroga* that when he felt that his end was very near, he would send him all of Christine Daaé's papers. This was his way of thanking the *daroga* for the kindness the Persian had once shown him. These papers had been written by Christine for Raoul, but she had left them with Erik with a few other small things. Erik said that the two had gone, intending to be married. He asked the Persian to inform the young couple of his death when he received Christine's papers, and to advertise it in the *Epoque*.

Darius helped Erik down to the street. A taxi was waiting for him. The Persian, who was at the window, heard Erik say, "Go to the Opera."

And the taxi drove off into the night.

The Persian had seen the poor, unfortunate Erik for the last time. Three weeks later, a notice in the *Epoque* read: "Erik is dead."

◆

It is now impossible to deny that the Phantom of the Opera did exist. There is so much proof of his existence that we can follow Erik's actions logically through the whole tragedy of the Chagnys.

The case greatly excited the capital, and Christine Daaé was represented as a poor girl caught between two brothers. Nobody suspected what really happened; nobody understood that Christine and Raoul had disappeared in order to enjoy a happiness which they did not want to make public after the mysterious death of Count Philippe. They went to Scandinavia— and maybe Madame Valérius, who disappeared at the same time, joined them there.

The newspapers continued to try to understand the mystery long after the unintelligent detective Faure gave up. Only the Persian knew the whole truth and held the main proofs which he received from Erik just before his death. I had the job of completing those proofs, and the *daroga* directed my inquiries. He told me where to gather information, who to speak to.

When I asked the Persian to tell me how Erik managed to take the money from Richard's pocket in spite of the safety pin, he reminded me that Erik was called "the trap door lover." He told me to look in the managers' office, which I later did, and there lay the trap door under the manager's desk.

The Persian's story, Christine Daaé's papers, and the statements made to me by people who worked under Richard and Moncharmin all helped me to make some important discoveries. I have not been able to find the house on the lake because Erik blocked all the entrances. On the other hand, I discovered secret passages, and the trap door that was used by the Persian and Raoul to enter the cellars.

According to the Persian, Erik was born in France in a small town near Rouen. He was born with a terrible face—no nose, yellow eyes—that he had to hide. He ran away and joined a fair, where he was shown to the public as the "the living dead." He crossed all of Europe, from fair to fair, and completed his education as an artist and magician with these traveling shows. He sang beautifully, practiced ventriloquism, and performed unbelievable tricks. When the Princess of Mazenderan in Persia heard about him, she instructed the *daroga* to find him and bring him to her.

His tricks were used for political murders and the king liked him. Erik had very original ideas about architecture and he built a palace full of trap doors and secret passages. The building was the work of a genius. The king did not want anyone else to have a palace like this, so he ordered that Erik and all the men who worked for him be put to death. The *daroga* was told to do the killing. Erik had once helped him, and the *daroga* repaid him by providing him with an escape. A body was later found, and because the king believed this to be Erik's, he did not have the *daroga* murdered. But the *daroga* was sent out of Persia, and he went to Paris.

Erik escaped to Constantinople, where he again built a great palace for the king there. Of course, he had to leave for the same reason he left Persia; he knew too much. He went to Paris, where he worked on building houses, and on the Opera. He dreamed of creating a place unknown to the rest of the earth, where he could hide from men's eyes for all time.

The reader knows and guesses the rest. Poor, unhappy Erik! Should we pity him? Should we curse him? I saw his skeleton the other day, when they took it from the spot where Christine had him buried. And what will they do with that skeleton? The best place for the skeleton of the Opera ghost is in the National School of Music. It is no ordinary skeleton.

ACTIVITIES

Chapters 1–3

Before you read

1 Do you believe in ghosts? What proof do people sometimes give for the existence of ghosts?

2 Read the Introduction to this book. Discuss why the Paris Opera was the perfect place for a horror story about the phantom of the Opera.

3 Answer these questions. Check the meanings of the words in *italics* in the Word List at the back of this book.

    a Can you name a famous *monster* from a book or movie?

    b Can you name a *genius* in each of these areas: science, literature, politics, sports, music?

    c What are people in your country often *superstitious* about?

    d Can you think of three uses for a *safety pin*?

    e Can you name a *ballet* and an *opera*? Do you know who wrote them?

    f In what part of a building do you expect to find:
      a *cellar*? a *chandelier*? a *trap door*?

    g What do *angels* look like? Where do they live? What kind of powers do they sometimes have in stories?

    h Draw one of these animals:
      a *toad* a *scorpion* a *grasshopper*

While you read

4 Write the names of the characters beside the notes.

    a retiring managers; lose money because
      of the Opera Ghost's demands   ....

    b main dancer of the ballet; responsible
      for the speech at the retirement ceremony   ....

    c the face of Death, with deep hollow eyes,
      yellow skin, no nose; uses Box Five   ....

    d in charge of moving scenery; dies
      early in the story   ....

e	box-keeper; receives money and little presents from the Opera Ghost	....
f	writer of *A Manager's Memories*; one of the new managers at the Opera	....
g	triumphs in the prison scene of *Faust*; has music lessons from the Angel of Music	....
h	a forty-one-year-old count; looks after his younger brother	....
i	a shy, twenty-one-year-old viscount; frightened almost to death in the graveyard at Perros-Guirec	....
j	one of the new managers of the Opera; a respected writer of music	....
k	a talented violinist; promises to send the Angel of Music to his daughter after his death	....
l	a music teacher; admires the musical talent of Christine and her father	....
m	sent to Christine by her father; turns people into musical geniuses	....

After you read

5 What happens in each of these places? Discuss why these events are important to the story.

   a La Sorelli's dressing room
   b the third cellar under the stage
   c Christine Daaé's dressing room after her triumph in *Faust*
   d the top floor of the Opera during the supper for the retiring managers
   e Box Five at the Opera when it is sold to members of the public
   f at the seaside in Perros-Guirec when Christine and Raoul are children
   g the graveyard beside the church at Perros-Guirec

6 What is the reaction of Monsieur Richard and Monsieur Moncharmin to:

  a the passage written in red ink in the memorandum book?

  b the letter from O.G.?

  c the letter from Monsieur Debienne and Monsieur Poligny?

  d Madame Giry's explanation for the strange events in Box Five?

Chapters 4–6

Before you read

7 If you were Monsieur Moncharmin or Monsieur Richard, would you want to watch a performance from Box five? Discuss why (not).

8 What do you know about the Opera Ghost? Make a list of his physical features.

While you read

9 Check (✓) the word that describes how the characters feel in these situations.

  a Madame Giry when Monsieur Richard kicks her out of his office

  1) angry .....   **2)** sad .....

  b Carlotta when she receives two letters in red ink

  1) frightened .....   **2)** confident .....

  c the new managers in Box Five at the end of Act I

  1) depressed .....   **2)** optimistic .....

  d Christine when she sees Viscount Chagny in the audience

  1) nervous .....   **2)** bold .....

  e Monsieur Moncharmin and Monsieur Richard when Carlotta sings like a toad

  1) confused .....   **2)** amused .....

  f Raoul during his conversation with Madame Valérius

  1) disappointed .....   **2)** emotional .....

10 Circle the right word.

    a Raoul buys a *white / red* mask to wear to the party at the Opera.

    b Christine is wearing a *white / black* mask at the party.

    c Raoul recognizes the face of Death because he saw it in a *theater / graveyard.*

    d Christine's voice changes when the man dressed as Red Death is *near / far away.*

    e In the private box Raoul cries because he thinks Christine *loves / lies to* him.

    f When Christine removes her mask in front of Raoul, her face looks *tragic / evil.*

    g A strange but beautiful male voice seems to lead Christine into a different world on the other side of her *curtain / mirror.*

    h Erik and the Angel of Music are *the same creature / two different creatures.*

11 Check (✓) the word that describes how Christine feels in these situations.

    a when she and Raoul pretend to have wedding plans

        1) cheerful .....   **2)** depressed .....

    b on the roof, wrapped in Raoul's arms

        1) courageous .....   **2)** anxious .....

    c when she first gets to know the Angel of Music

        1) excited .....   **2)** annoyed .....

    d when Erik takes her across the lake to a room filled with flowers

        1) calm .....   **2)** amazed .....

    e when Erik wants her to sing something from the Opera with him

        1) insulted .....   **2)** loving .....

    f when she tears off Erik's mask

        1) affectionate .....   **2)** desperate .....

After you read

12 Who receive letters from O.G. in Chapter 4? What demands do they contain?

13 What three names is the Phantom of the Opera known by?

14 What makes us think that the Phantom is in these places?

    a in Box Five after the second act of *Faust*

    b at the masked party at the Opera

    c two floors above the masked party when Christine and Raoul are in a private box

    d in Christine's dressing room at two o'clock

    e in the opera house when Raoul is listening to Christine who is on stage again in Carlotta's place

    f inside the Opera when Raoul and Christine go for walks

    g under the roof of the Opera

    h in Christine's dressing room after the chandelier falls

    i at the lake under the opera house

15 Work with another student. Act out one of these conversations.

    a Carlotta talking to one of her loyal supporters about the two letters in red ink that she has received

    b Raoul telling Philippe about the party at the Opera, including the Red Death, the mysterious voice, and Christine's mirror

    c Erik's mother telling her husband about their new-born baby

Chapters 7–9

Before you read

16 What do you think the storm at the end of Chapter 6 represents?

17 Discuss Christine's mixed feelings about Erik.

While you read

18 Mark each statement T (true) or F (false).

    a The Persian is one of Raoul's closest friends.   .....

    b Raoul keeps a gun in his bedroom.   .....

    c Raoul and Philippe have different opinions about the wisdom of Raoul's wedding plans.   .....

    d Gabriel, Mercier, and Rémy are employed at the the Paris Opera.   .....

    e Monsieur Moncharmin and Monsieur Richard are in the audience when Christine disappears.   .....

    f Madame Giry leaves the opera house when Christine disappears.   .....

    g Monsieur Mifroid can give orders because he works for the police.   .....

19 Complete each sentence with one word.

a O.G. wants the managers to put his 20,000 francs in an
....

b Monsieur Moncharmin and Monsieur Richard suspect that
Madame Giry is .... O.G.'s allowance.

c The managers walk .... so that no one can take the
20,000 francs from Monsieur Richard's coat pocket.

d Monsieur Moncharmin uses a .... pin to guarantee
that the money stays in his partner's pocket.

e At midnight the managers discover that Monsieur Richard's
pocket is ....

20 Mark each statement T (true) or F (false).

a Raoul tells Monsieur Moncharmin and Monsieur
Richard that Christine has disappeared.   .....

b Monsieur Mifroid persuades Raoul to believe that
Philippe has taken Christine away.   .....

c Raoul trusts the Persian because the Persian knows
that Erik is real and dangerous.   .....

d The Persian hates Erik and wants to harm him.   .....

e The Persian uses a magic trick to allow him and
Raoul to walk through the mirror.   .....

f The torture room is in Erik's house.   .....

After you read

21 Explain what causes these characters to act in these odd ways.

a Raoul shoots his gun at two eyes at the foot of his bed.

b Raoul stands during Christine's performance in *Faust*.

c The new managers shout for a safety pin.

d These two managers won't let anyone touch them, and they
walk backward.

e Christine disappears in the middle of her performance.

f Mauclair seems to fall asleep while he's working.

22 Why are these important to the story?

   a the key to a gate in Rue Scribe

   b the lost gold ring

   c a newspaper report of a promise of marriage

   d total darkness during the performance of *Faust*

   e 20,000 francs in false bills

   f the mirror in Christine's dressing room

23 What does Raoul learn about Erik from the Persian?

Chapters 10–12

Before you read

24 Discuss these questions.

   a Why does Erik have a torture room in his house?

   b How will the story end for the Persian, Raoul, Christine, and Erik? Can you imagine a good ending and a bad ending for each of them?

While you read

25 Match each of these with Erik's purpose for it.

a the singing lake	.....	**1)** to look like a normal person
b walls built of hollow bricks	.....	**2)** to enter his house
c a trap door	.....	**3)** to kill people
d a stone in a wall	.....	**4)** to charm people and then to drown them
e the Punjab rope and the torture room	.....	**5)** to hide the people in the torture room
f a new mask	.....	**6)** to make his voice carry into Christine's room
g the bag of life and death	.....	**7)** to hold his keys
h a trick forest	.....	**8)** to enter the opera house cellars

26 What can the Persian and Raoul see, hear, and feel in the torture room? Write the words SEE, HEAR, and FEEL.

a Erik's laugh ....

b a body being dragged along the floor ....

c an iron tree with painted leaves ....

d scratches on the mirrors ....

e burning heat ....

f lions and other dangerous animals ....

g rain ....

h a Punjab rope ....

i a black nail ....

j cool air ....

k stairs leading to a cellar ....

l the hands on Raoul's watch ....

27 In which order is Erik in these places? Write the numbers 1–6.

a the National School of Music, Paris .....

b Constantinople .....

c a small town near Rouen, France .....

d the Opera, Paris .....

e Persia .....

f towns and cities around Europe .....

After you read

28 Discuss these questions.

a What effect does Christine's kindness to Erik have on his actions? How does this save the lives of Raoul and the Persian? How does it lead to Erik's death?

b In the story Erik is described as a genius. What are his talents?

c Why have the Persian and Erik continued a kind of friendship over the years?

29 Why does the author not tell the events of the story in the order they happen? Why does he use letters, parts of Moncharmin's book, and the results of his own findings to tell the story? Do you think it is a good way to tell the story?

Writing

30 You are a journalist who writes about music, especially about opera. Write a report for your newspaper about Christine Daaé's triumph in *Faust* when she sings in place of Carlotta.

31 Write Christine's words when she prayed to her dead father in the graveyard at Perros-Guirec.

32 You are the Persian. Write a letter to Erik before Christine disappears from the stage of the opera house and warn him of the dangers involved in being in love with Christine Daaé. Suggest a better life for Erik away from the Paris Opera.

33 The author has seen Christine's papers, in which she wrote down everything that happened to her. Choose one event and write her description of it.

34 Write about the mysterious death of Count Philippe for the newspaper *Epoque*. Where was his body found, and what do the police suspect happened?

35 You are Raoul. Write a description of the torture room, how you felt in there, and what you thought would happen.

36 You are Madame Valérius and you have moved to Scandinavia with Christine and Raoul. Write a letter to your sister in Paris and tell her about your life with the young couple.

37 If you could interview one character from the story, who would you like to question? Write the questions you would ask.

38 At the end of the story, the author asks the reader, "Should we pity him? Should we curse him?" What do you think? Why?

39 Write a book report. What do you like about this book and what do you not like? Do you recommend it?

Answers for the Activities in this book are available from the Penguin Readers website. A free Activity Worksheet is also available from the website. Activity Worksheets are part of the Penguin Teacher Support Programme, which also includes Progress Tests and Graded Reader Guidelines. For more information, please visit: www.penguinreaders.com.

WORD LIST

allowance (n) money that you are given regularly or for a special reason

angel (n) a spiritual being, believed to be God's servant or messenger in Heaven; a very kind and special person

ballet (n) a type of dancing done on a theater stage, in which a story is told through music and dance, not words

box (n) a separate area like a little room in a theater from which a small number of people can watch the performance

box office (n) a place in a theater where tickets are sold

carriage (n) a vehicle pulled by horses

cellar (n) a room under a building

chandelier (n) a large decoration which hangs from the ceiling, made of pieces of glass that hold lights

count (n) a man with a high social position in Europe because of the family he comes from

divine (adj) with the qualities of God

franc (n) old French money, which is not in use now

genius (n) great and unusual ability; a person with that ability

grasshopper (n) an insect with long back legs that can jump high into the air

mask (n) something that covers all or part of your face to protect or hide it

memorandum (n) a short, official note written to another person in the same organization

monster (n) an extremely cruel and evil person

opera (house) (n) a building in which musical plays and other kinds of entertainment are performed for the public

phantom (n) a ghost

safety pin (n) a bent metal pin used to fasten things, with a cover for its point so it cannot hurt anyone

scorpion (n) a creature like an insect that has a poisonous sting in its curved tail

skeleton (n) all the bones in a person's or animal's body

skull (n) the bones of a person's or animal's head

superstitious (adj) believing that some objects or actions are lucky or unlucky

toad (n) a brownish animal that lives near water and has long legs for jumping

torture (n) extreme pain over a long period of time, usually caused to punish someone or get information from them

trap door (n) a small door that covers an opening in a floor or ceiling

tremble (v) to shake because you are worried, afraid, or excited

triumph (n/v) an important success, especially after a difficult struggle

ventriloquist (n) someone who speaks without moving their lips, so the sound seems to come from somewhere else

viscount (n) a man with a high social position in Britain because of the family he comes from